TURKISH

PHRASEBOOK & DICTIONARY

Contacting the Editors

Every effort has been made to provide accurate information in this publication, but changes are inevitable. The publisher cannot be responsible for any resulting loss, inconvenience or injury. We would appreciate it if readers would call our attention to any errors or outdated information. We also welcome your suggestions; if you come across a relevant expression not in our phrase book, please contact us at: **hello@insightguides.com**

First Edition: 2016
Printed in China

Cover & Interior Design: Pawel Pasternak
Production: AM Services
Production Manager: Vicky Glover
Cover Photo: Shutterstock

Interior Photos: Shutterstock

CONTENTS

INTRODUCTION

Pronunciation	7	Grammar	12
How to use the App	10		

GETTING STARTED

THE BASICS	**20**	NEED TO KNOW	28
NUMBERS	**20**	Border Control	28
NEED TO KNOW	20	**MONEY**	**30**
Ordinal Numbers	22	NEED TO KNOW	30
Time	23	At the Bank	31
NEED TO KNOW	23	**CONVERSATION**	**33**
Days	24	NEED TO KNOW	33
NEED TO KNOW	24	Language Difficulties	35
Dates	24	Making Friends	36
Months	25	Travel Talk	38
Seasons	26	Personal	39
Holidays	26	Work & School	40
ARRIVAL & DEPARTURE	**28**	Weather	41

EXPLORING

GETTING AROUND	**44**	Taxi	60
NEED TO KNOW	44	Bicycle & Motorbike	62
Tickets	45	Car Hire	62
Airport Transfer	48	Fuel Station	64
Checking In	50	Asking Directions	65
Luggage	51	Parking	67
Finding your Way	52	Breakdown & Repair	68
Train	53	Accidents	68
Departures	55	**PLACES TO STAY**	**69**
On Board	55	NEED TO KNOW	69
Bus	56	Somewhere to Stay	70
Metro	57	At the Hotel	72
Boat & Ferry	58	Price	74

Preferences	74	Social Media	89
Questions	74	Phone	90
Problems	77	Telephone Etiquette	92
Checking Out	78	Fax	93
Renting	79	Post	93
Domestic Items	81	**SIGHTSEEING**	**95**
At the Hostel	82	NEED TO KNOW	95
Going Camping	83	Tourist Information	96
COMMUNICATIONS	**85**	On Tour	96
NEED TO KNOW	85	Seeing the Sights	98
Online	86	Religious Sites	100

ACTIVITIES

SHOPPING	**104**	Newsagent & Tobacconist	121
NEED TO KNOW	104	Photography	122
At the Shops	105	Souvenirs	123
Ask an Assistant	107	**SPORT & LEISURE**	**127**
Personal Preferences	108	NEED TO KNOW	127
Paying & Bargaining	109	Watching Sport	128
Making a Complaint	110	Playing Sport	129
Services	111	At the Beach/Pool	130
Hair & Beauty	112	Winter Sports	132
Antiques	114	Out in the Country	134
Clothing	114	**TRAVELING**	
Colors	115	**WITH CHILDREN**	**137**
Clothes & Accessories	116	NEED TO KNOW	137
Fabric	119	Out & About	137
Shoes	120	Baby Essentials	138
Sizes	120	Babysitting	141

HEALTH & SAFETY

EMERGENCIES	**144**	NEED TO KNOW	148
NEED TO KNOW	144	Finding a Doctor	148
POLICE	**146**	Symptoms	149
NEED TO KNOW	146	Conditions	151
Crime & Lost Property	146	Treatment	151
HEALTH	**148**	Hospital	152

Dentist	153	Basic Supplies	158
Gynecologist	154	Child Health	
Optician	155	& Emergency	160
Payment & Insurance	155	**DISABLED TRAVELERS**	**161**
PHARMACY	**156**	NEED TO KNOW	161
NEED TO KNOW	156	Asking for Assistance	162
What to Take	157		

FOOD & DRINK

EATING OUT	**166**	Meat & Poultry	182
NEED TO KNOW	166	Vegetables & Staples	185
Where to Eat	167	Fruit	188
Reservations		Cheese	189
& Preferences	168	Dessert	189
How to Order	170	Sauces & Condiments	190
Cooking Methods	172	At the Market	191
Dietary Requirements	173	In the Kitchen	194
Dining With Children	175	**DRINKS**	**196**
How to Complain	175	NEED TO KNOW	196
Paying	176	Non-alcoholic Drinks	198
MEALS & COOKING	**177**	Aperitifs, Cocktails	
Breakfast	178	& Liqueurs	199
Appetizers	179	Beer	200
Soup	180	Wine	200
Fish & Seafood	180	**ON THE MENU**	**202**

GOING OUT

GOING OUT	**218**	NEED TO KNOW	222
NEED TO KNOW	218	The Dating Game	222
Entertainment	219	Accepting & Rejecting	224
Nightlife	220	Getting Intimate	225
ROMANCE	**222**	Sexual Preferences	225

DICTIONARY

ENGLISH-TURKISH	**228**	**TURKISH-ENGLISH**	**256**

PRONUNCIATION

This section is designed to familiarize you with the sounds of Turkish using our simplified phonetic transcription. You'll find the pronunciation of the Turkish letters explained below, together with their 'imitated' equivalents. To use this system, found throughout the phrase book, simply read the pronunciation as if it were English, noting any special rules below.

Letters underlined in the transcriptions should be read with slightly more stress, but don't overdo this as Turkish is not a heavily stressed language.

CONSONANTS

Letter	Approximate Pronunciation	Symbol	Example	Pronunciation
c	like j in jam	j	ceket	*jeh • keht*
ç	like ch in church	ch	kaç	*kahch*
g	like g in ground	g	gitmek	*geet • mehk*
ğ	1. at the end of a word, it lengthens the preceding vowel		dağ	*dah**
	2. a silent letter between vowels		kağıt	*kah • iht*
	3. after e, like y in yawn	y	değer	*deh • yehr*
h	like h in hit	h	mahkeme	*mah • keh • meh*
j	like s in pleasure	zh	bagaj	*bah • gahzh*
r	trilled r	r	tren	*trehn*
s	like s in sit	s	siyah	*see • yahh*
ş	like sh in shut	sh	şişe	*shee • sheh*

Letters b, d, f, k, l, m, n, p, t, v, y and z are pronounced as in English.
*Bold indicates a lengthening of the sound, an extra emphasis on the vowel sound.

ⓘ

Turkish consonants are typically shorter and harder-sounding than English consonants. When reading Turkish words, be sure to pronounce all the letters.

VOWELS

Letter	Approximate Pronunciation	Symbol	Example	Pronunciation
a	like a in father	ah	kara	kah • rah
e	like e in net	eh	sene	seh • neh
ı	similar to i in ill	ih	tatlı	taht • lih
i	like ee in see	ee	sim	seem
o	like o in spot	oh	otel	oh • tehl
ö	similar to ur in fur	ur	börek	bur • rehk
u	like oo in cool	oo	uzak	oo • zahk
ü	like ew in few	yu	üç	yuch

ⓘ

Turkish vowels are quite different from English vowels. As with consonants, they are generally shorter and harder than English vowels. In the pronunciation guide, certain vowels are followed by an 'h' to emphasize the shortness of the sound.

DIPHTHONGS

Letter	Approximate Pronunciation	Symbol	Example	Pronunciation
ay	like ie in tie	ie	bay	bie
ey	like ay in day	ay	bey	bay
oy	like oy in boy	oy	koy	koy

Türkçe (Turkish) is the native language of some 70 million inhabitants of the Republic of Turkey, and is spoken by large numbers of ethnic Turks living outside of Turkey. The Turkish alphabet used today dates only from 1928, when Atatürk, the founder of Modern Turkey, chose to replace the Ottoman script that had been used for centuries.

Turkish differs from English in two important ways. First, affixes take the place of many words that, in other languages, would be written separately (such as pronouns, negatives and prepositions); these affixes are attached to a base word. Second, it features 'vowel harmony'; this restricts which vowels may appear within a word. So, while affixes in their standard forms have the vowel 'i' or 'e', this may change when the affix is attached to another word. For example, the suffix **in** (´s) stays **in** in **evin** (the house's), but becomes **un** in **memurun** (the official's) and **ün** in **gözün** (the eye's).

HOW TO USE THE APP

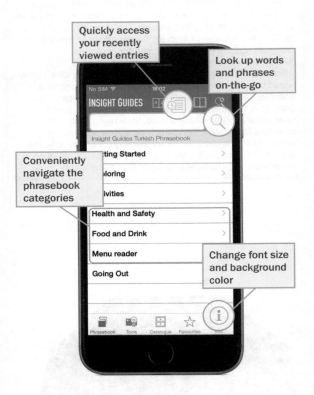

Quickly access your recently viewed entries

Look up words and phrases on-the-go

Conveniently navigate the phrasebook categories

Change font size and background color

No SIM 📶   18:02

INSIGHT GUIDES

Insight Guides Turkish Phrasebook

Getting Started   >

Exploring   >

Activities   >

Health and Safety   >

Food and Drink   >

Menu reader

Going Out

Phrasebook   Tools   Catalogue   Favourites   Info

Save the most useful
everyday words and
phrases to your Favorites

Use the Flash
Cards Quiz to learn
and memorize new
words easily

Take all digital
advantages of the app:
listen to words and
phrases pronounced
by native speakers

Is there a traditional Turkish/
an inexpensive restaurant near
here?

Yakınlarda geleneksel Türk
yemekleri/ucuz yemek suna
bir lokanta var mı?

*yah·kihn·lahr·dah
geh·leh·nehk·sehl tyurk
yeh·mehk·leh·ree/oo·jooz
yeh·mehk soo·nahn beer
loh·kahn·tah vahr mih*

Can you reco...   A table for......

Phrasebook   Tools   Catalogue   Favourites   Info

To learn how to
activate the app,
see the inside
back cover of this
phrasebook.

GRAMMAR

REGULAR VERBS

Turkish verbs use a stem with suffixes that change according to what tense (present, past, future) and person they indicate. The stem of the verb can be found by removing **mak** or **mek** from the infinitive of the verb, e.g. the stem of **gezmek** (to travel) is **gez**; the stem of **açmak** (to open) is **aç**. The past tense has the suffix **–d–**, and the future, the suffix **–ecek–**.

GEZMEK (TO TRAVEL)		PRESENT	PAST	FUTURE
I	**ben**	gez**erim**	gez**dim**	gez**eceğim**
you (*sing., inf.*)	**sen**	gez**ersin**	gez**din**	gez**eceksin**
he/she/it	**o**	gez**er**	gez**di**	gez**ecek**
we (*pl./form.*)	**biz**	gez**eriz**	gez**dik**	gez**eceğiz**
you	**siz**	gez**ersiniz**	gez**diniz**	gez**eceksiniz**
they	**onlar**	gez**erler**	gez**diler**	gez**ecekler**

To form the present continuous tense (which can also be used to express the future tense), the suffix **-iyor** is added to the stem, followed by the endings for each person, i.e. **-um**, **-un**, etc. (see below).

GEZMEK (TO TRAVEL)		PRESENT CONTINOUS	PAST	FUTURE
I	**ben**	gez**iyorum**	gez**iyordum**	gez**iyor olacağım**
you (*sing., inf.*)	**sen**	gez**iyorsun**	gez**iyordun**	gez**iyor olacaksın**
he/she/it	**o**	gez**iyor**	gez**iyordu**	gez**iyor olacak**
we	**biz**	gez**iyoruz**	gez**iyorduk**	gez**iyor olacağız**

| you (pl./form.) | **siz** | gez**i**yorsunuz | ez**i**yordunuz | gez**i**yor olacaksınız |
| they | **onlar** | gez**i**yorlar | gez**i**yorlardı | gez**i**yor olacaklar |

IRREGULAR VERBS

Turkish is rather remarkable among living languages in having a highly regular verb conjugation system. A minor irregularity is found in thirteen verbs where the present general takes a vowel-harmony congruent vowel after the root that is in the **i/ü** series, rather than the **a/e** series, which is the standard. These are used regularly on a day-to-day basis and are best learned by heart.

INFINITIVE	PRESENT SIMPLE	
almak	**alır**	to take/get
bulmak	**bulur**	to find
durmak	**durur**	to stop/to halt
kalmak	**kalır**	to remain/to stay
olmak	**olur**	to be/to become
sanmak	**sanır**	to suppose
varmak	**varır**	to arrive
vurmak	**vurur**	to strike/to hit
bilmek	**bilir**	to know how to
gelmek	**gelir**	to come
görmek	**görür**	to see
ölmek	**ölür**	to die
vermek	**verir**	to give

The rich system of suffixes that are added at the end of verb stems to express tense, person and manner is remarkably regular and uniform in Turkish.

To express the English 'have/has,' you use the word with its possessive ending, followed by the word **-var** meaning 'exists':

I have a car.   **Arabam var.**
                                 (literally, 'my car exists')

He/She has a bicycle.   **Bisikleti var.**
                                (literally, 'his/her bicycle
                                exists')

To say 'don't/doesn't have' the word **yok** is used instead of **var**:
I don't have a ticket.   **Biletim yok.**
                                (literally, 'my ticket exists-not')
He/She doesn't have any money. **Parası yok.**
                                (literally, 'his/her money exists-
                                not')

WORD ORDER

Standard word order in Turkish is subject-object-verb. For
instance:
Murat kedileri gördü.   Murat saw the cats.
Murat=subject, kedileri=object, gördü=verb.
Questions are formed either with question words:

ne	what
kim	who
nerede	where
nasıl	how
niçin	why

Or, the question particle **mi** is appended after the word that is
the focus of the question:

Murat kedileri gördü mü?   Did Murat see the cats?
Murat kedileri mi gördü?   Did Murat see the cats?
Murat mı kedileri gördü?   Was it Murat who saw the cats?

NEGATIONS

The letter **–m–** , added between the verb stem and what follows,
indicates negation. Some examples:
He/She travels.   **Gezer.**   He/She does not travel.   **Gezmez.**
He/She is traveling.   **Geziyor.**   He/She is not traveling.   **Gezmiyor.**

IMPERATIVES

The imperative for second person singular is simply the verbal stem. The negative imperative is the same with the **–m–** suffix.

Come! (one person)   **Gel!**
Don't come! (one person)   **Gelme!**

The positive and negative imperatives for second person plural or formal are the same pair, with the plural suffix:

Come! (several persons)   **Gelin!**
Don't come! (several persons) **Gelmeyin!**

NOUNS & ARTICLES

Nouns in Turkish change their ending according to their function in a sentence. These grammatical case endings are themselves subject to change due to vowel harmony. For beginners, it is often difficult to separate the case endings from the other suffixes added to a word and, therefore, it is better to learn words within a complete phrase.

Nouns do not have grammatical gender. The indefinite demonstrative article **bir** (literally, 'one') corresponds closely to the English 'a/an', however there is no definite article corresponding to the English 'the'. This article is generally conveyed by the demonstrative adjectives **bu/şu** (this) and **o** (that).

ADJECTIVES

Adjectives come before the noun, and there are no case or singular/plural endings on them:

uzun yol   long road
uzun yollar   long roads
Uzun yoldan geldim.   I arrived from a long trip.
                          (Literally: I arrived from a long road.)

PRONOUNS

The challenge for English speakers is to know when to use
sen and **siz**, both of which are 'you' in English. It is clear that a
group of people must be addressed with **siz**, the second person
plural pronoun. However, this same pronoun, like in some other
languages, is used as a respectful form of address for unfamiliar,
elderly or hierarchically higher individuals. For the tourist, it is
safe to address people with **siz**, until familiarity develops or all
agree to use the less formal **sen**. The latter form, **sen**, is the
correct form to use among family members, good friends and
with children.

I	**ben**
you (*sing., inf.*)	**sen**
he/she/it	**o**
we	**biz**
you (*pl./form.*)	**siz**
they	**onlar**

COMPARATIVES & SUPERLATIVES

The comparative is generally formed with **daha** (more); it
precedes the adjective. Example:

büyük	big
daha büyük	bigger

The preferred way for conveying the sense of 'less' is again
through the use of **daha** with the adjective that has the opposite
meaning.

küçük	small
daha küçük	smaller

The superlative is formed by adding **en** in front of the adjective:

en büyük	the biggest
en küçük	the smallest

ADVERBS & ADVERBIAL EXPRESSIONS

Almost any adjective can be used as an adverb that modifies a verb:

güzel konuştu	he spoke beautifully
yavaş/süratli sürün!	Drive slowly/quickly!

Adverbs precede the verb or the adjective they qualify, and they take no case or singular/plural endings:

hızlı koşmak	to run fast
koyu mavi gözler	intensely blue eyes

Adverbs may be directional or time-related, or they may qualify the verb:

içeri	inside
ileri	forward
erken	early
geç	late
çok	a lot, too much
az	a little, too little
hemen	right away

The **ca/ce** suffix forms adverbs from adjectives or nouns:

sinsice	sneakily
kahramanca	heroically

Examples with some of the foregoing:

içeri girin!	Go inside!
çok yedim	I ate too much
erken gelin!	Come early!
sinsice yürüyor	he is walking sneakily
hemen yaparlar	They will do it right away

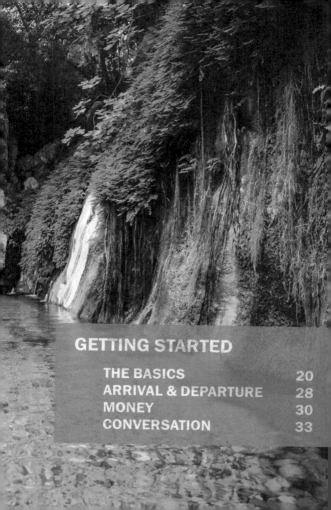

GETTING STARTED

THE BASICS   20
ARRIVAL & DEPARTURE   28
MONEY   30
CONVERSATION   33

THE BASICS

NUMBERS

NEED TO KNOW

0	**sıfır**
	sih • fihr
1	**bir**
	beer
2	**iki**
	ee • _kee_
3	**üç**
	yuch
4	**dört**
	durrt
5	**beş**
	behsh
6	**altı**
	ahl • _tih_
7	**yedi**
	yeh • _dee_
8	**sekiz**
	seh • _keez_
9	**dokuz**
	doh • _kooz_
10	**on**
	ohn
11	**on bir**
	ohn beer

12	**on iki**
	ohn ee • kee
13	**on üç**
	ohn yuch
50	**elli**
	ehl • lee
60	**altmış**
	ahlt • mihsh
70	**yetmiş**
	yeht • meesh
80	**seksen**
	sehk • sehn
90	**doksan**
	dohk • sahn
100	**yüz**
	yyuz
101	**yüz bir**
	yyuz beer
200	**ikiyüz**
	ee • kee yyuz
500	**beşyüz**
	behsh yyuz
1,000	**bin**
	been
10,000	**on bin**
	ohn been
1,000,000	**bir milyo**
	beer meel • yohn

ORDINAL NUMBERS

first	**birinci** *bee • reen • <u>jee</u>*
second	**ikinci** *ee • keen • <u>jee</u>*
third	**üçüncü** *yu • chyun • <u>jyu</u>*
fourth	**dördüncü** *durr • dyun • <u>jyu</u>*
fifth	**beşinci** *beh • sheen • <u>jee</u>*
once	**bir kere** *<u>beer</u> keh • reh*
twice	**iki kere** *ee • <u>kee</u> keh • reh*
three times	**üç kere** *<u>yuch</u> keh • reh*

TIME

NEED TO KNOW

What time is it?	**Saat kaç?** *sah • aht kahch*
It's noon [midday].	**Saat on iki.** *sah • aht on ee • kee*
At midnight.	**Gece yarısı.** *geh • jeh yah • rih • sih*
From nine o'clock to 5 o'clock.	**Saat dokuzdan beşe.** *sah • aht doh • kooz • dahn beh • sheh*
Twenty after [past] four.	**Dördü yirmi geçiyor.** *durr • dyu yeer • mee geh • chee • yohr*
A quarter to nine.	**Dokuza çeyrek var.** *doh • koo • zah chay • rehk vahr*
5:30 a.m./p.m.	**Öğleden önce/sonra beş buçuk.** *ur • leh • dehn urn • jeh/ sohn • rah behsh boo • chook*

DAYS

NEED TO KNOW

Monday	**Pazartesi** *pah • zahr • teh • see*
Tuesday	**Salı** *sah • lih*
Wednesday	**Çarşamba** *chahr • shahm • bah*
Thursday	**Perşembe** *pehr • shehm • beh*
Friday	**Cuma** *joo • mah*
Saturday	**Cumartesi** *joo • mahr • teh • see*
Sunday	**Pazar** *pa • zar*

DATES

yesterday	**dün** *dyun*
today	**bugün** *boo • gyun*
tomorrow	**yarın** *yah • rihn*
day	**gün** *gyun*
week	**hafta** *hahf • tah*
month	**ay** *ie*
year	**yıl** *yihl*

Turkey follows a day-month-year format instead of the month-day-year format used in the U.S.
For example, July 25, 2008; **25/07/08** = 7/25/2008 in the U.S.

MONTHS

January	**Ocak** *oh • jahk*
February	**Şubat** *shoo • baht*
March	**Mart** *mahrt*
April	**Nisan** *nee • sahn*
May	**Mayıs** *mah • yihs*
June	**Haziran** *hah • zee • rahn*
July	**Temmuz** *tehm • mooz*
August	**Ağustos** *ah • oos • tohs*
September	**Eylül** *ay • lyul*
October	**Ekim** *eh • keem*
November	**Kasım** *kah • sihm*
December	**Aralık** *ah • rah • lihk*

SEASONS

spring	**ilkbahar**
	eelk • bah • hahr
summer	**yaz**
	yahz
fall [autumn]	**sonbahar**
	sohn • bah • hahr
winter	**kış**
	kihsh

HOLIDAYS

January 1, New Year's Day	**Yılbaşı**
April 23, National Independence and Children's Day	**Ulusal Egemenlik ve Çocuk Bayramı**
May 19, Commemoration of Atatürk's Landing in Samsun and Youth and Sports Day	**Atatürk'ü Anma, Gençlik ve Spor Bayramı**
August 30, National Independence Victory Day	**Zafer Bayramı**
October 29, Republic Day	**Cumhuriyet Bayramı**
Festival of Sweetmeats (at the end of Ramadan)	**Şeker Bayramı**

Festival of Sacrifice (approx 70 days after Ramadan)	**Kurban Bayramı**

August 30th, Victory Day, memorializes the final victory that brought the War of Independence to an end in 1922. October 29th is the anniversary of the founding of the Turkish Republic in 1923.

The Festival of Sweetmeats and the Festival of Sacrifice are Muslim holidays whose dates are based on the lunar calendar, rather than the Gregorian calendar. The Festival of Sweetmeats is a three-holiday to mark the end of the month of Ramadan. The name marks the tradition of visiting friends and family with a gift of 'sweetmeats.'

The Festival of Sacrifice is a four-day holiday that commemorates the willingness of Abraham to sacrifice his son for Allah. It is celebrated by the sacrifice of an animal followed by a family feast and donations of food to the poor.

April 23rd, National Sovereignty and Children's Day, is the anniversary of the opening of the Grand National Assembly, which happened in Ankara in 1920. Traditionally this is a holiday dedicated to children. May 19th, the Commemoration of Atatürk's Landing in Samsun, Youth and Sports Day, commemorates the start of the Turkish War of Independence, which began in 1919. Now this holiday is dedicated to youth and sports.

ARRIVAL & DEPARTURE

NEED TO KNOW

I'm here on vacation [holiday]/business.	**Tatil/İş için buradayım.** *tah • teel/eesh ee • cheen boo • rah • dah • yihm*
I'm going to...	**...gidiyorum.** *...gee • dee • yoh • room*
I'm staying at the...Hotel.	**...otelinde kalıyorum.** ... *oh • teh • leen • deh ah • lih • yoh • room*

BORDER CONTROL

I'm just passing through.	**Sadece geçiyorum.** *sah • deh • jeh geh • chee • yoh • room*
I would like to declare...	**...beyan etmek istiyorum.** *...beh • yahn eht • mehk ees • tee • yoh • room*
I have nothing to declare.	**Beyan edeceğim birşey yok.** *beh • yahn eh • deh • jeh • yeem beer shay yohk*

YOU MAY HEAR...

Lütfen, biletiniz/pasaportunuz.
lyut • fehn bee • leh • tee • neez/
pah • sah • pohr • too • nooz

Your ticket/
passport please.

Ziyaret sebebiniz nedir?
zee • yah • reht seh • beh • bee • neez
neh • deer

What's the
purpose of
your visit?

Nerede kalıyorsunuz?
neh • reh • deh
kah • lih • yohr • soo • nooz

Where are you
staying?

Ne kadar kalacaksınız?
neh kah • dahr kah • lah • jak • sih • nihz

How long are
you staying?

Kiminlesiniz?
kee • meen • leh • see • neez

Who are you
with?

Gümrüğe tabi eşyanız var mı?
gyum • ryu • yeh tah • bee
ehsh • yah • nihz vahr mih

Do you have
anything to
declare?

Bunun için gümrük vergisi ödemeniz gerekir.
boo • noon ee • cheen gyum • ryuk
vehr • gee • see ur • deh • meh • neez
geh • reh • keer

You must pay
duty on this.

Lütfen şu çantayı açınız.
lyut • fehn shoo
chahn • tah • yih ah • chih • nihz

Please open
that bag.

YOU MAY SEE...

GÜMRÜK	customs
VERGİSİZ EŞYALAR	duty-free goods
BEYAN EDECEK EŞYASI OLANLAR	passengers with goods to declare
BEYAN EDECEK EŞYASI OLMAYANLAR	passengers with nothing to declare
PASAPORT KONTROLU	passport control
POLİS	police

MONEY

NEED TO KNOW

Where's…?	**…nerede?** …_neh_ • _reh_ • _deh_
the ATM	**Paramatik** _pah_ • _rah_ • _mah_ • _teek_
the bank	**Banka** _bahn_ • _kah_
the currency exchange office	**Döviz bürosu** _dur_ • _veez byu_ • _roh_ • _soo_
What time does the bank open/close?	**Banka saat kaçta açılıyor/kapanıyor?** _bahn_ • _kah sah_ • _aht kach_ • _tah_ _ah_ • _chih_ • _lih_ • _yohr/kah_ • _pah_ • _nih_ • _yohr_
I'd like to change dollars/pounds into lira.	**Dolar/İngiliz Sterlini bozdurmak istiyorum.** _doh_ • _lahr/een_ • _gee_ • _leez stehr_ • _lee_ • _nee_ _bohz_ • _door_ • _mahk ees_ • _tee_ • _yoh_ • _room_
I want to cash some traveler's checks [cheques].	**Seyahat çekleri bozdurmak istiyorum.** _seh_ • _yah_ • _haht chek_ • _leh_ • _ree_ _bohz_ • _door_ • _mahk ees_ • _tee_ • _yoh_ • _room_

AT THE BANK

Can I exchange foreign currency here?	**Burada döviz bozdurabilir miyim?** _boo_ • rah • dah dur • _veez_ bohz • doo • rah • bee • _leer_ mee • yeem
What's the exchange rate?	**Döviz kuru nedir?** dur • _veez_ koo • _roo_ neh • deer
How much is the fee?	**Ne kadar komisyon alıyorsunuz?** _neh_ kah • dahr koh • mees • _yohn_ ah • _lih_ • yohr • soo • nooz
I've lost my traveler's checks [cheques].	**Seyahat çeklerimi kaybettim.** seh • yah • _haht_ chehk • leh • ree • _mee_ _kie_ • beht • teem
My credit card was lost.	**Kredi kartım kayboldu.** _kreh_ • dee kahr • _tihm kie_ • bohl • doo
My credit cards have been stolen.	**Kredi kartlarım çalındı.** _kreh_ • dee kahrt • lah • _rihm_ chah • lihn • _dih_
My card doesn't work.	**Kartım çalışmıyor.** kahr • _tihm_ chah • _lihsh_ • mih • yohr

For Numbers, see page 20.

YOU MAY SEE...

The monetary unit is the Turkish Lira (**Türk Lirası**, abbreviated **TL.**) One TL is divided into one hundred **yeni kuruş**, abbreviated **Kr.**
Coins: 1, 5, 10, 25, 50 **Kr** and **1 TL**
Notes: 5, 10, 20, 50 and 100 **TL**

At some banks, cash can be obtained from ATMs with Visa™, Eurocard™, American Express® and many other international cards. Instructions are often given in English. Banks with a **Change** sign will exchange foreign currency. You can also change money at travel agencies and hotels, but the rate will not be as good. Remember to bring your passport when you want to change money.

YOU MAY SEE...

KARTI TAK	insert card
İPTAL ET	cancel
SİL	clear
GİR	enter
PİN NUMARASI	PIN
ÇEKİLEN PARALAR	withdraw funds
CARİ HESAPTAN	from checking [current] account
TASARRUF HESABINDAN	from savings account
FATURA	receipt

Banka (the bank) and **postahane** (the post office) are good options for exchanging currency. **Döviz bürosu** (currency exchange offices) are also located in many tourist centers, though if you decide to change money in an exchange office, look around for the best rate and keep your eye on the commission. Also, remember to bring your passport, in case you are asked for identification.

CONVERSATION

NEED TO KNOW

Hello.	**Merhaba.** _mehr_ • hah • bah
Hi!	**Selam!** seh • _lahm_
How are you?	**Nasılsınız?** _nah_ • sihl • sih • nihz
Fine, thanks.	**İyiyim, teşekkürler.** ee • _yee_ • yeem teh • shehk • kyur • _lehr_
Excuse me!	**Afedersiniz!** _ahf_ • eh • dehr • see • neez
Do you speak English?	**İngilizce biliyor musunuz?** een • gee • _leez_ • jeh bee • _lee_ • yohr moo • soo • nooz
What's your name?	**İsminiz nedir?** ees • mee • _neez neh_ • deer
My name is...	**İsmim...** ees • _meem_...
Pleased to meet you.	**Tanıştığımıza memnun oldum.** tah • nihsh • tih • ih • mih • _zah_ mehm • _noon_ ohl • doom
Where are you from?	**Nerelisiniz?** _neh_ • reh • lee • see • neez
I'm from the U.S./ U.K.	**Amerikadanım/Birleşik Krallıktanım.** ah • meh • _ree_ • kah • dah • nihm/ beer • leh • _sheek_ krahl • lihk • _tah_ • nihm
What do you do?	**Ne iş yapıyorsunuz?** _neh_ eesh yah • _pih_ • yohr • soo • nooz

I work for...	**...için çalışıyorum.**
	...ee • <u>cheen</u> chah • lih • <u>shih</u> • yoh • room
I'm a student.	**öğrenciyim.**
	ur • rehn • <u>jee</u> • eem
I'm retired.	**Emekliyim.**
	eh • mehk • <u>lee</u> • yeem
Do you like...?	**...sever misiniz?**
	...seh • <u>vehr</u> mee • see • neez
Goodbye. (said by departing persons)	**Hoşçakalın.**
	hosh • <u>chah</u> kah • lihn
Goodbye. (said by second person staying behind)	**Güle güle.**
	gyu • <u>leh</u> gyu • <u>leh</u>
See you later.	**Tekrar görüşmek üzere.**
	tehk • <u>rahr</u> gur • ryush • <u>mehk</u> yu • zeh • reh

When formally addressing someone, it is polite to use the person's first name followed by either **Hanım** (polite address for women) or **Bey** (polite address for men). So Ali and his wife Binnur would be addressed as Ali Bey and Binnur Hanım, respectively. **Bay** (polite address for male foreigners) and **Bayan** (polite address for female foreigners) are also used, particularly for non-Muslims. In business settings, **Sayin** (polite address for men and women in a business setting) is commonly used followed by the last name. For example, Ali Kandemir would be addressed as Sayin Kandemir.

LANGUAGE DIFFICULTIES

Do you speak English?	**İngilizce biliyor musunuz?**
	een • gee • leez • jeh bee • lee • yohr moo • soo • nooz
Does anyone here speak English?	**Burada İngilizce konuşan biri var mı?**
	boo • rah • dah een • gee • leez • jeh koh • noo • shahn bee • ree vahr mih
I don't speak Turkish.	**Türkçe bilmiyorum.**
	tyurk • cheh beel • mee • yoh • room
Can you speak more slowly?	**Daha yavaş konuşur musunuz lütfen?**
	dah • hah yah • vahsh koh • noo • shoor moo • soo • nooz lyut • fehn
Can you repeat that?	**Tekrar eder misiniz lütfen?**
	tekh • rahr eh • dehr mee • see • neez lyut • fehn
Excuse me?	**Efendim?**
	eh • fehn • deem
What was that?	**O neydi?**
	oh nay • dee
Write it down, please.	**Lütfen yazar mısınız.**
	lyut • fehn yah • zahr mih • sih • nihz

Can you translate this for me?	**Bunu benim için tercüme eder misiniz?**
	boo • noo beh • neem ee • cheen
	tehr • jyu • meh eh • dehr mee • see • neez
What does this/that mean?	**Bu/O ne demek?**
	boo/oh neh deh • mehk
I understand.	**Anladım.**
	ahn • lah • dihm
I don't understand.	**Anlamadım.**
	ahn • lah • mah • dihm
Do you understand?	**Anladınız mı?**
	anh • lah • dih • nihz mih

YOU MAY HEAR...

Sadece çok az İngilizce konuşuyorum.
sah • deh • jeh chohk ahz
een • geh • leez • jeh
koh • noo • shoo • yoh • room

I only speak
a little English.

İngilizce konuşmuyorum.
een • gee • leez • jeh
koh • noosh • moo • yoh • room

I don't speak
English.

MAKING FRIENDS

Hello.	**Merhaba.**
	mehr • hah • bah
Hi!	**Selam!**
	seh • lahm
Good morning.	**Günaydın.**
	gyu • nie • dihn
Good afternoon.	**İyi günler.**
	ee • yee gyun • lehr

Good evening.	**İyi akşamlar.**
	ee • <u>yee</u> ahk • <u>shahm</u> • lahr
My name is…	**İsmim…**
	ees • <u>meem</u>…
What's your name?	**İsminiz nedir?**
	ees • mee • <u>neez</u> neh • deer
I'd like to introduce you to…	**Sizi…ile tanıştırmak istiyorum.**
	see • <u>zee</u>…ee • <u>leh</u>
	tah • nihsh • tihr • <u>mahk</u>
	ees • <u>tee</u> • yoh • room
Nice to meet you.	**Tanıştığımıza memnun oldum.**
	tah • nihsh • tih • ih • mih • <u>zah</u>
	mehm • <u>noon</u> ohl • doom
How are you?	**Nasılsınız?**
	<u>nah</u> • sihl • sih • nihz
Fine, thanks.	**İyiyim, teşekkürler.**
	ee • <u>yee</u> • yeem teh • shehk • kyur • <u>lehr</u>
And you?	**Siz?**
	seez

(i)

Turkish has both a formal 'you,' **siz**, and an informal 'you', **sen**. The formal 'you' is used when speaking with strangers and out of respect, for example, when talking with someone older than you. The informal 'you' can be used with people you know or people younger than you. Though older people maintain this distinction, many young people start using the informal 'you' right away.

TRAVEL TALK

I'm here...	**...amacıyla buradayım.**
	...ah • mah • _jihy_ • lah boo • rah • dah • yihm
on business	**İş**
	eesh
on vacation	**Tatil**
	tah • _teel_
studying	**Okumak**
	oh • koo • _mahk_
I'm staying for...	**...için kalıyorum.**
	...ee • _cheen_ kah • _lih_ • yoh • room
I've been here...	**...burdayım.**
	...boor • _dah_ • yihm
a day	**Bir gündür**
	beer _gyun_ • dyur
a week	**Bir haftadır**
	beer hahf • _tah_ • dihr
a month	**Bir aydır**
	beer _ie_ • dihr
Where are you from?	**Nerelisiniz?**
	neh • reh • lee • see • neez
I'm from...	**...denim.**
	..._deh_ • neem

For Numbers, see page 20.

PERSONAL

Who are you with?	**Kiminlesiniz?**
	kee • _meen_ • leh • see • neez
I'm on my own.	**Tek başımayım.**
	tehk bah • shih • _mah_ • yihm
I'm with...	**...ile birlikteyim.**
	...ee • _leh_ beer • leek • _teh_ • yeem
my husband/wife	**Kocam/Karım**
	koh • _jahm_/kah • _rihm_
my boyfriend/ girlfriend	**Erkek/Kız arkadaşım**
	ehr • _kehk_/kihz ahr • kah • dah • shihm
a friend	**Bir arkadaş**
	beer ahr • kah • _dahsh_
a colleague	**Bir meslektaş**
	beer mehs • lehk • _tahsh_
When's your birthday?	**Doğum gününüz ne zaman?**
	doh • _oom_ gyu • nyu • _nyuz_ neh zah • mahn
How old are you?	**Kaç yaşındasınız?**
	kahch yah • shihn • _dah_ • sih • nihz
I'm...	**...yaşındayım.**
	...yah • shihn • _dah_ • yihm
Are you married?	**Evli misiniz?**
	ehv • _lee_ mee • see • neez
I'm single.	**Bekârım.**
	beh • _kah_ • rihm
I'm married.	**Evliyim.**
	ehv • _lee_ • yeem
I'm divorced.	**Boşanmışım.**
	boh • shan • _mih_ • shihm
I'm separated.	**Ayrıyım.**
	ie • _rih_ • yihm
I'm in a relationship.	**Beraberliğim var.**
	beh • rah • behr • lee • _eem_ vahr

I'm widowed.	**Dulum.** _doo_ • loom
Do you have children/grandchildren?	**Çocuğunuz/Torununuz var mı?** choh • joo • oo • _nooz_/ toh • roo • noo • _nooz_ vahr mih

WORK & SCHOOL

What do you do?	**Ne iş yapıyorsunuz?** _neh_ eesh yah • _pih_ • yohr • soo • nooz
What are you studying?	**Ne okuyorsunuz?** _neh_ oh • _koo_ • yohr • soo • nooz
I'm studying…	**…okuyorum.** …oh • _koo_ • yoh • room
I work full/part time.	**Tam/Yarım zamanlı çalışıyorum.** tahm/yah • _rihm_ zah • mahn • lih chah • lih • shih • yoh • room
I'm between jobs.	**İşten yeni ayrıldım.** eesh • _tehn_ yeh • _nee_ ie • rihl • _deem_
I work at home.	**Evde çalışıyorum.** ehv • _deh_ chah • lih • _shih_ • yoh • room
Who do you work for?	**Kimin için çalışıyorsunuz?** kee • _meen_ ee • cheen chah • lih • _shih_ • yohr • soo • nooz

I work for...	**...için çalışıyorum.**
	...ee • cheen chah • lih • shih • yoh • room
Here's my business card.	**Buyrun, kartvizitim.**
	booy • roon cahrt • vee • zee • teem

WEATHER

What is the weather forecast for tomorrow?	**Yarın için hava tahmini nasıl?**
	yah • rihn ee • cheen hah • vah tah • mee • nee nah • sihl
What beautiful/ terrible weather!	**Ne kadar güzel/kötü bir hava!**
	neh kah • dahr gyu • zehl/ kur • tyu beer hah • vah
It's cool/warm.	**Serin/Ilık.**
	seh • reen/ih • lihk
It's rainy/sunny.	**Yağmurlu/Güneşli.**
	yah • moor • loo/gyu • nehsh • lee
It's snowy/icy.	**Karlı/Buzlu.**
	kahr • lih/booz • loo
Do I need a jacket/ an umbrella?	**Monta/Şemsiyeye ihtiyacım var mı?**
	mohn • tah/shehm • see • yeh • yeh eeh • tee • yah • jihm vahr mih

For Seasons, see page 26.

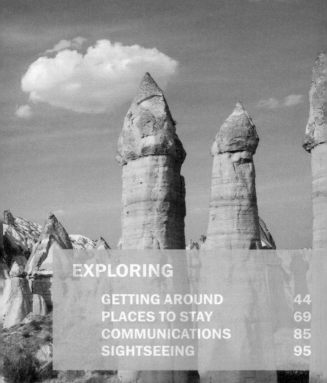

EXPLORING

GETTING AROUND	44
PLACES TO STAY	69
COMMUNICATIONS	85
SIGHTSEEING	95

GETTING AROUND

NEED TO KNOW

How do I get to town?	**Şehire nasıl gidebilirim?** sheh • hee • <u>reh nah</u> • sıhl gee • deh • bee • <u>lee</u> • reem
Where's...?	**...nerede?** ...<u>neh</u> • reh • deh
the airport	**Havaalanı** hah • <u>vah</u> • ah • lah • nıh
the train [railway] station	**Tren garı** <u>trehn</u> gah • <u>rih</u>
the bus station	**Otobüs garajı** oh • toh • <u>byus</u> gah • rah • <u>jih</u>
the subway [underground] station	**Metro istasyonu** <u>meht</u> • roh ees • tahs • yoh • <u>noo</u>
How far is it?	**Ne kadar uzakta?** <u>neh</u> kah • dahr oo • zahk • <u>tah</u>
Where can I buy tickets?	**Nereden bilet alabilirim?** <u>neh</u> • reh • dehn bee • <u>leht</u> ah • lah • bee • <u>lee</u> • reem

A one-way [single]/ round-trip [return] ticket.	**Sadece gidiş/gidiş dönüş bileti.** _sah • deh • jeh gee • deesh/ gee • deesh dur • nyush bee • leh • tee_
How much?	**Ne kadar?** _neh kah • dahr_
Are there any discounts?	**İndirim var mı?** _een • dee • reem vahr mih_
Which...?	**Hangi...?** _hahn • gee..._
gate	**kapı** _kah • pih_
lane	**hat** _haht_
platform	**peron** _peh • rohn_
Where can I get a taxi?	**Nerede taksi bulabilirim?** _neh • reh • deh tahk • see boo • lah • bee • lee • reem_
Please take me to this address.	**Lütfen beni bu adrese götürün.** _lyut • fehn beh • nee boo ahd • reh • seh gur • tyu • ryun_
Where can I rent a car?	**Nereden bir araba kiralayabilirim?** _neh • reh • dehn beer ah • rah • bah kee • rah • lah • yah • bee • lee • reem_
Can I have a map?	**Bir harita alabilir miyim?** _beer hah • reeh • tah ah • lah • bee • leer mee • yeem_

TICKETS

When's...to Istanbul?	**İstanbul'a...ne zaman?** _ees • tahn • boo • lah...neh zah • mahn_
the (first) bus	**(ilk) otobüs** _(eelk) oh • toh • byus_

the (next) flight	**(bundan sonraki) uçak**
	(boon • dahn sohn • rah • kee) oo • chahk
the (last) train	**(son) tren**
	(sohn) trehn
Where can I buy tickets?	**Nereden bilet alabilirim?**
	neh • reh • dehn bee • leht ah • lah • bee • lee • reem
One ticket/two tickets, please.	**Bir/İki bilet lütfen.**
	beer/ee • kee bee • leht lyut • fehn
For today/tomorrow.	**Bugün/Yarın.**
	boo • gyun/yah • rihn
A one-way [single]/return ticket.	**Sadece gidiş/gidiş dönüş bileti.**
	sah • deh • jeh gee • deesh/gee • deesh dur • nyush bee • leh • tee
A first/economy class ticket.	**Birinci sınıf/Ekonomi sınıfı bileti.**
	bee • reen • jee sih • nihf/eh • koh • noh • mee sih • nih • fih bee • leh • tee
How much?	**Ne kadar?**
	neh kah • dahr
Is there a discount for…?	**…için indirim var mı?**
	…ee • cheen een • dee • reem vahr mih
children	**Çocuklar**
	choh • jook • lahr
students	**Öğrenciler**
	ur • rehn • jee • lehr
senior citizens	**Yaşlılar**
	yash • lih • lahr
I have an e-ticket.	**Bir e-biletim var.**
	beer eh • bee • leh • teem vahr
Can I buy a ticket on the bus/train?	**Otobüste/Trende bir bilet alabilir miyim?**
	oh • toh • byu • steh/trehn • deh beer bee • leht ah • lah • bee • leer • mee • yeem

Can I return on the same ticket?	**Aynı biletle dönebilir miyim?** *ie • nih bee • leht • leh* *dur • nee • bee • leer mee • yeem*
I'd like to…my reservation.	**Reservasyonumu…istiyorum.** *reh • zehr • vahs • yoh • noo • <u>moo</u>…* *ees • tee • yoh • room*
cancel	**iptal etmek** *eep • <u>tahl</u> eht • <u>mehk</u>*
change	**değiştirmek** *deh • yeesh • teer • <u>mehk</u>*
confirm	**teyit etmek** *teh • <u>yeet</u> eht • <u>mehk</u>*
Do I have to stamp the ticket before boarding?	**Binmeden önce biletimi mühürletmem gerekiyor mu?** *been • meh • dehn ohn • jeh* *bee • leh • tee • mih* *myu • huhr • leht • mehm* *geh • reh • kee • yohr • moo*
How long is this ticket valid?	**Bilet ne kadar zaman geçerli?** *bee • leht neh kah • dahr* *zah • mahn geh • chehr • lee*

For Days, see page 24.

YOU MAY HEAR…

Hangi havayoluyla uçuyorsunuz?
<u>hahn</u> • gee hah • <u>vah</u> yoh • <u>looy</u> • lah
oo • <u>choo</u> • yohr • soo • nooz

What airline are you flying?

İç/Dış hatlar mı?
eech/<u>dihsh</u> haht • <u>lahr</u> mih

Domestic/ International?

Hangi terminal?
<u>hahn</u> • gee tehr • mee • nahl

What terminal?

	Kapılar Gates	**201-218**
	Kapılar Gates	**301-312**
🍴	**Restoranlar** Food court	
	Mescit Masjid	♿ **WC** **Toilets**
$€£ ₤¥	**Change -Exchange**	**Tax Free**
	Gümrüksüz Satış Mağazaları Duty Free Shops	

AIRPORT TRANSFER

How much is a taxi to the airport?	**Havaalanına bir taksi ne kadar?** _hah • vah • ah • lah • nih • nah beer_ _tahk • see neh kah • dahr_
To...Airport, please.	**...havaalanına lütfen.** _...hah • vah • ah • lah • nih • nah lyut • fehn_
My airline is...	**Havayolum...** _hah • vah • yoh • loom..._
My flight leaves at...	**Uçağım saat...kalkacak.** _oo • chah • ihm sah • aht...kahl • kah • jahk_
I'm in a rush.	**Acelem var.** _ah • jeh • lehm vahr_
Can you take an alternate route?	**Alternatif bir yol kullanabilir misiniz?** _ahl • tehr • nah • teef beer yohl_ _kool • lah • nah • bee • leer mee • see • neez_
Can you drive faster/slower?	**Daha hızlı/yavaş kullanabilir misiniz?** _dah • hah hihz • lih/yah • vash_ _kool • lah • nah • bee • leer mee • see • neez_

For Time, see page 23.

YOU MAY HEAR...

Bir sonraki!
beer sohn • rah • kee

Next!

Lütfen, biletiniz/pasaportunuz.
yut • fehn bee • leh • tee • neez/
pah • sah • pohr • too • nooz

Your ticket/
passport, please.

Kaç parça bavulunuz var?
kach pahr • chah bah • voo • loo • nooz
vahr

How much
luggage do you
have?

Bavul ağırlığınız fazla.
bah • vool ah • ihr • lih • ih • nihz fahz • lah

You have
excess luggage.

El çantası için o çok ağır/büyük.
ehl chahn • tah • sih ee • cheen oh
chohk ah • ihr/byu • yuhk

That's too
heavy/large
for a carry-on
[to board].

Bu çantaları kendiniz mi hazırladınız?
boo chan • tah • lah • rih kehn • dee • neez
mee hah • zihr • lah • dih • nihz

Did you pack
these bags
yourself?

Taşımanız için herhangi bir şey verildi mi?
tah • shih • mah • nihz ee • cheen
hehr • hahn • gee beer shay
veh • reel • dee mee

Did anyone give
you anything to
carry?

Ceplerinizi boşaltın.
jehp • leh • ree • nee • zee boh • shahl • tihn

Empty your
pockets.

Ayakkabılarınızı çıkarın.
ah • yahk • kah • bih • lah • rih • nih • zih
chih • kah • rihn

Take off your
shoes.

Şu anda kalkan uçak...
shoo ahn • dah kahl • kahn oo • chahk...

Now boarding
flight...

CHECKING IN

Where is check-in?	**Kayıt masası nerede?** *kah • yiht mah • sah • sih neh • reh • deh*
My name is...	**İsmim...** *ees • meem...*
I'm going to...	**...gidiyorum.** *...gee • dee • yoh • room*
I have...	
one suitcase	**Bir tane bavulum var** *beer tah • neh bah • voo • loom vahr*
two suitcases	**İki tane bavulum var** *ee • kee tah • neh bah • voo • loom vahr*
one piece of hand luggage	**Bir tane el bagajım var** *beer tah • neh ehl bah • gah • zhihm vahr*
How much luggage is allowed?	**Ne kadar bavula izin var?** *neh kah • dahr bah • voo • lah ee • zeen vahr*
Which gate does flight...leave from?	**...numaralı uçak hangi biniş kapısından hareket edecek?** *...noo • mah • rah • lih oo • chahk hahn • gee bee • neesh kah • pih • sihn • dahn hah • reh • keht eh • deh • jehk*
I'd like a window/an aisle seat.	**Pencere/Koridor kenarı istiyorum.** *pehn • jeh • reh/ koh • ree • dor keh • nah • rih ees • tee • yoh • room*
When do we leave/ arrive?	**Ne zaman ayrılıyoruz/varıyoruz?** *neh zah • man ie • rih • lih • yoh • rooz/ vah • rih • yoh • rooz*
Is there any delay on flight...?	**...uçuşunda herhangi bir gecikme var mı?...** *oo • choo • shoon • dah hehr • hahn • gee beer geh • jeek • meh vahr mih*

How late will it be? **Ne kadar gecikecek?**
neh kah • dahr geh • jee • keh • jehk

YOU MAY SEE... 👁

VARIŞ	arrivals
GİDİŞ	departures
BAVUL TESLİM BANDI	baggage claim
İÇ HAT UÇUŞLARI	domestic flights
DIŞ HAT UÇUŞLARI	international flights
UÇUŞ KAYDI MASASI	check-in desk
E-BİLET KAYDI	e-ticket check-in
ÇIKIŞ KAPILARI	departure gates

LUGGAGE

Where is/are...?	**...nerede?**
	...<u>neh</u> • reh • deh
the luggage carts [trolleys]	**El arabaları**
	ehl ah • rah • bah • lah • <u>rih</u>
the luggage lockers	**Bagaj dolapları**
	bah • <u>gahj</u> doh • lahp • lah • <u>rih</u>
the baggage claim	**Bavul teslim bandı**
	bah • <u>vool</u> tehs • <u>leem</u> bahn • dih
My luggage has been lost.	**Bavulumu kaybettim.**
	bah • voo • loo • <u>moo kie</u> • beht • teem
My luggage has been stolen.	**Bavulum çalındı.**
	bah • voo • <u>loom</u> chah • lihn • <u>dih</u>
My suitcase was damaged.	**Bavulum hasar görmüş.**
	bah • voo • <u>loom</u> hah • <u>sahr</u> gurr • <u>myush</u>

FINDING YOUR WAY

Where is/are...?	**...nerede?**	
	neh • reh • deh	
the currency	**Döviz bürosu**	
exchange office	*dur • veez byu • roh • soo*	
the car rental	**Araba kiralama**	
	ah • rah • bah kee • rah • lah • mah	
the exit	**Çıkış**	
	chih • kihsh	
the taxis	**Taksiler**	
	tahk • see • lehr	
Is there...into town?	**Kente...var mı?**	
	kehn • teh...vahr mih	
a bus	**otobüs**	
	oh • toh • byus	
a train	**tren**	
	trehn	
a Metro	**metro**	
	meht • roh	

For Asking Directions, see page 65.

YOU MAY SEE...

PERONLARA	to the platforms
DANIŞMA	information
YER AYIRTMA	reservations
VARIŞ	arrivals
ÇIKIŞ	departures

TRAIN

How do I get to the train station?	**Tren garına nasıl gidebilirim?**
	trehn gah • rih • nah nah • sihl gee • deh • bee • lee • reem
Is it far?	**Uzak mı?**
	oo • zahk mih
Where is/are...?	**...nerede?**
	...neh • reh • deh
the ticket office	**Bilet gişesi**
	bee • leht gee • sheh • see
the luggage lockers	**Bagaj dolapları**
	bah • gahj doh • lahp • lah • rih
the platforms	**Peronlar**
	peh • rohn • lahr
Could I have a schedule [timetable], please?	**Lütfen, bir tren tarifesi alabilir miyim?**
	lyut • fehn beer trehn tah • ree • feh • see ah • lah • bee • leer mee • yeem

> (i)
>
> The **Türkiye Cumhuriyeti Devlet Demiryolları (TCDD)** (Turkish Republic State Railways) operates in most regions of the country. Trains with sleeping cars are a good option for a long, overnight trip. For international travel, there are a number of express trains with separate first- and second-class cars. The cost of tickets for each differs by about 30%. For reduced rates on international travel, purchase an InterRail pass or a Balkan Flexipass. For domestic travel, be sure to inquire about train stops. Express trains generally connect large cities, while commuter trains are slower and make various stops along the route. Reservations may be made in advance via the TCDD website at www.tcdd.gov.tr.

How long is the trip?	**Yolculuk ne kadar sürüyor?**
	yohl • joo • look neh kah • dahr
	syu • ryu • yohr
Do I have to change trains?	**Aktarma yapmak gerekiyor mu?**
	ahk • tahr • mah yahp • mahk
	geh • reh • kee • yohr moo

For Tickets, see page 45.

YOU MAY HEAR...

Lütfen yerlerinizi alın!
lyut • fehn yehr • leh • ree • nee • zee
ah • lihn

All aboard!

Biletler lütfen.
bee • leht • lehr lyut • fehn

Tickets, please.

...aktarma yapmanız gerek.
...ahk • tahr • mah yahp • mah • nihz
geh • rehk

You have to change at...

Bir sonraki durak...
beer sohn • rah • kee doo • rahk...

Next stop...

DEPARTURES

Which platform does the train to...leave from?	**...giden tren hangi perondan kalkıyor?** *...gee • <u>dehn</u> trehn hahn • <u>gee</u> peh • rohn • <u>dahn</u> kahl • <u>kih</u> • yohr*
Is this the platform to...?	**...treni bu perondan mı kalkıyor?** ... *treh • <u>nee</u> boo peh • rohn • <u>dahn</u> mih kahl • <u>kih</u> • yohr*
Where is platform...?	**...peronu nerede?** *...peh • roh • <u>noo</u> <u>neh</u> • reh • deh*
Where do I change for...?	**...için nerede aktarma yapacağım?** *...ee • cheen <u>neh</u> • reh • deh ahk • tahr • <u>mah</u> yah • pah • jah • <u>yihm</u>*

ON BOARD

Is this seat taken?	**Bu koltuk dolu mu?** *boo kohl • <u>took</u> doh • <u>loo</u> moo*
I think that's my seat.	**Bu koltuk benim.** *boo kohl • <u>took</u> beh • <u>neem</u>*
Here's my reservation.	**Buyrun rezervasyonum.** *booy • roon reh • zehr • vahs • yoh • noom*

BUS

(i)

Turkish city buses are very inexpensive. Destinations are usually posted on the bus itself, but double check with the driver before boarding. In Istanbul, green buses are reserved for commuters and require payment in special tokens. Orange buses are public and tickets can be purchased on board. In Istanbul, it is a good idea to purchase an **akbil** (smart ticket) which allows you to buy credit to pay for bus, sea and subway/tunnel travel. Paying with an **akbil** gets you a discount of between 10-25%.

(eye symbol)

YOU MAY SEE...

OTOBÜS DURAĞI	bus stop
GİRİŞ/ÇIKIŞ	enter/exit
BİLETİNİZİ MÜHÜRLETİN	stamp your ticket

Where's the bus station?	**Otobüs garajı nerede?**
	oh • toh • _byus_ gah • rah • _jih_ _neh_ • reh • deh
How far is it?	**Ne kadar uzakta?**
	neh kah • dahr oo • zahk • _tah_
How do I get to...?	**...nasıl gidebilirim?**
	...nah • sihl gee • deh • bee • _lee_ • reem
Does the bus stop at...?	**Otobüs...duruyor mu?**
	oh • toh • _byus_...doo • _roo_ • yohr moo
Could you tell me when to get off?	**İneceğim yeri söyler misiniz?**
	ee • neh • jeh • _yeem_ yeh • _ree_ sur • _ylehr_ mee • see • neez

Do I have to change buses!	**Aktarma yapmam gerekiyor mu?**
	ahk • tahr • <u>mah</u> yahp • <u>mahm</u>
	geh • reh • <u>kee</u> • yohr moo
Stop here, please!	**Burada durun lütfen!**
	boo • rah • <u>dah doo</u> • roon <u>lyut</u> • fehn

For Tickets, see page 45.

METRO

(i)

Metro transportation is an option in Ankara and
Istanbul. **Tünel** (Tunnel), the second-oldest metro
in the world, first used in 1875, is located in Istanbul and
travels between the Karaköy and Beyoğlu stations. Paying by
akbil (smart ticket) will get you a discount on both metro and
Tünel travel in Istanbul.

Where's the metro station?	**En yakın metro istasyonu nerede?**
	ehn yah • <u>kihn meht</u> • roh
	ees • tah • syoh • <u>noo neh</u> • reh • deh

Can I have a map of the metro?	**Bir metro planı verir misiniz?** *beer <u>meht</u> • roh plah • <u>nih</u> veh • <u>reer</u> mee • see • neez*
Which line for…?	**…için hangi hattı kullanmam gerekiyor?** *…ee • <u>cheen hahn</u> • gee haht • <u>tih</u> kool • lahn • <u>mahm</u> geh • reh • <u>kee</u> • yohr*
Where do I change for…?	**…gitmek için nerede tren değiştirmeliyim?** *…geet • mehk ee • cheen neh • reh • deh <u>trehn</u> deh • yeesh • teer • meh • <u>lee</u> • yeem*
Is this the right train for…?	**Bu tren…gidiyor mu?** *boo trehn…gee • <u>dee</u> • yohr moo*
How many stops to…?	**… kaç durak var?** *kach doo • rahk vahr*
Where are we?	**Neredeyiz?** *<u>neh</u> • reh • deh • yeez*

For Finding your Way, see page 52.

BOAT & FERRY

When is the ferry to…?	**…araba vapuru saat kaçta?** *…ah • rah • <u>bah</u> vah • poo • <u>roo</u> sah • <u>aht</u> kahch • <u>tah</u>*
Where are the life jackets?	**Can yelekleri neredeler?** *jahn yeh • lehk • leh • ree <u>neh</u> • reh • deh • ler*
What time is the next sailing?	**Bir sonraki sefer saat kaçta?** *beer sohn • rah • kee seh • fehr sah • aht kach • tah*
Can I book a seat/cabin?	**Bir yer/kabin ayırtabilir miyim?** *beer yehr/kah • been ah • yihr • tah • bee • leer mee • yeem*

How long is the crossing?

Sefer ne kadar sürüyor?
seh • fehr neh kah • dahr syu • ryu • yohr

For Weather, see page 41.

YOU MAY SEE...

CANKURTARAN SANDALI	life boats
CAN YELEĞİ	life jackets

Turkey is essentially surrounded by water. That, combined with Turkey's habitual road traffic, makes boat travel an important alternative. The country's most important port is in Istanbul. **İstanbul Deniz Otobüsleri (IDO)** (Istanbul Sea Bus Company) provides regular catamaran and ferry service around Istanbul. Catamarans are generally more comfortable and faster, though it is more expensive to take a catamaran than a ferry. **Denizline** operates between Istanbul and Izmir and a number of operators provide ferry and car ferry service between Çeşme and Brindisi and Ancona, Italy. There are also a number of connections between Turkey and the Aegean Islands in summertime. **Akbil** (smart ticket) can also be used for sea travel, giving you a discount of between 10-25% on your travel.

TAXI

Turkish taxis are generally yellow, marked with the word **taksi** (taxi) on top and have a letter 'T' on their license plates. Make sure that the meter is set to the correct rate: **gündüz** (day), from 6 a.m. to midnight, and **gece** (night), from midnight to 6 a.m. If you want to tip the driver, you can round up the fare. **Dolmuş** (group taxis) are an alternative to regular taxis. They follow specific routes, much like a bus, but stop as requested. They are cheaper than individual taxis.

Where can I get a taxi?	**Nerede taksi bulabilirim?** _neh_ • reh • deh tahk • _see_ boo • lah • bee • _lee_ • reem
I'd like a taxi now/ for tomorrow at…	**Şimdi/Yarın saat…için bir taksi istiyorum.** _sheem_ • dee/yah • _rihn_ sah • _aht_… ee • _cheen_ beer tahk • _see_ ees • _tee_ • yoh • room

Can you send a taxi?	**Bir taksi yollayabilir misiniz?**
	beer tahk • see yol • lah • yah • bee • leer
	mee • see • neez
Pick me up at....	**Beni...al.**
	beh • nee...teh ahl
Please take me to...	**Beni...götürür müsünüz lütfen.**
	beh • nee... gur • tyu • ryur
	myu • syu • nyuz lyut • fehn
this address	**bu adrese**
	boo ahd • reh • seh
the airport	**havaalanına**
	hah • vah • ah • lah • nih • nah
the train station	**tren garına**
	trehn gah • rih • nah
I'm late.	**Geciktim.**
	geh • jeek • teem
Can you drive faster/ slower?	**Daha hızlı/yavaş kullanabilir misiniz?**
	dah • hah hihz • lih/yah • vahsh
	kool • lah • nah • bee • leer mee • see • neez
Stop/Wait here.	**Burada durun/bekleyin.**
	boo • rah • dah doo • roon/
	behk • leh • yeen
How much will it cost?	**Ne kadar tutar?**
	neh kah • dahr too • tahr
You said...lira.	**Siz...lira dediniz.**
	seez...lee • rah deh • dee • neez
Keep the change.	**Üstü kalsın.**
	yus • tyu kahl • sihn
A receipt, please.	**Fatura lütfen.**
	fah • too • rah lyut • fehn

YOU MAY HEAR...

Nereye?
neh • reh • yeh

Adres nedir?
ahd • _rehs_ _neh_ • deer

Where to?
What's the address?

BICYCLE & MOTORBIKE

I'd like to rent [hire]...	**Bir...kiralamak istiyorum.**
	beer...kee • rah • lah • _mahk_
	ees • _tee_ • yoh • room
a bicycle	**bisiklet**
	bee • seek • _leht_
a moped	**mopet**
	moh • _peht_
a motorcycle	**motorsiklet**
	moh • tohr • seek • _leht_
How much per day/ week?	**Günlüğü/Haftalığı ne kadar?**
	gyun • lyu • _yu_/hahf • tah • lih • _ih_
	neh kah • dahr
Can I have a helmet/ lock?	**Kask/Kilit alabilir miyim?**
	kahsk/kee • _leet_
	ah • lah • bee • _leer_ mee • yeem

CAR HIRE

Where can I rent [hire] a car?	**Nereden bir araba kiralayabilirim?**
	neh • reh • dehn beer ah • rah • _bah_
	kee • rah • lah • _yah_ • bee • _lee_ • reem
I'd like to rent [hire]...	**Bir...kiralamak istiyorum.**
	beer...kee • rah • lah • _mahk_
	ees • tee • _yoh_ • room

a 2-/4-door car	**iki/dört kapılı araba**
	ee • kee/durrt kah • pih • lih ah • rah • bah
an automatic car	**otomatik araba**
	oh • toh • mah • teek ah • rah • bah
a car with air conditioning	**klimalı araba**
	klee • mah • lih ah • rah • bah
a car seat	**araba koltuğu**
	ah • rah • bah kohl • too • oo
How much...?	**...ne kadar?**
	...neh kah • dahr
per day/week	**Günlüğü/Haftalığı**
	gyun • lyu • yu/hahf • tah • lih • ih
per kilometer	**Kilometre başına**
	kee • loh • meht • reh bah • shih • nah
for unlimited mileage	**Sınırsız yakıt kullanımı**
	sih • nihr • sihz yah • kiht kool • lah • nih • mih
with insurance	**Sigortalı**
	sih • gohr • tah • lih
Are there any special weekend rates?	**Hafta sonu için indirim var mı?**
	hahf • tah soh • noo ee • cheen een • dee • reem vahr mih

YOU MAY HEAR...

Uluslararası sürücü belgeniz var mı?
oo • loos • _lahr_ • ah • rah • sih
syu • ryu • _jyu_ behl • geh • _neez_ vahr mih

Do you have an international driver's license?

Lütfen pasaportunuz.
lyut • fehn pas • sah • pohr • too • _nooz_

Your passport, please.

Sigorta istiyor musunuz?
sih • _gohr_ • tah ees • _tee_ • yohr
moo • soo • nooz

Do you want insurance?

...ön ödeme var.
..._urn_ ur • deh • _meh_ vahr

There is a deposit of...

Burasını imzalayınız.
boo • rah • sih • _nih_
eem • zah • _lah_ • yih • nihz

Please sign here.

FUEL STATION

Where's the fuel station, please?	**Benzin istasyonu nerede lütfen?** behn • _zeen_ ees • tah • syoh • _noo_ neh • reh • deh _lyut_ • fehn
Fill it up, please.	**Depoyu doldurun lütfen.** deh • poh • _yoo_ dohl • _doo_ • roon _lyut_ • fehn
...liters, please.	**...litre lütfen.** ..._lee_ • treh _lyut_ • fehn
I'll pay in cash/by credit card.	**Nakit/Kredi kartı ile ödeyeceğim.** nah • _keet_/kreh • _dee_ kahr • _tih_ ee • leh ur • deh • yeh • _jeh_ • yeem

For Numbers, see page 20.

YOU MAY SEE...

NORMAL	regular
SÜPER	premium [super]
DİZEL	diesel

ASKING DIRECTIONS

Is this the right road to...?	**Bu,...giden yol mu?**
	boo...gee • dehn yohl moo
How far is it to...?	**...buradan ne kadar uzakta?**
	...boo • rah • dahn neh kah • dahr oo • zahk • tah
Where's...?	**...nerede?**
	...neh • reh • deh
...Street	**...caddesi**
	...jahd • deh • see
this address	**Bu adres**
	boo ahd • rehs
the highway [motorway]	**Otoyol**
	oh • toh • yohl

Can you show me on the map? **Bana haritada gösterebilir misiniz?**
bah • nah hah • ree • tah • dah
gurs • teh • reh • bee • leer mee • see • neez

I'm lost. **Kayboldum.**
kie • bohl • doom

YOU MAY HEAR...

doğru ilerde *doh • roo ee • lehr • deh*	straight ahead
solda *sohl • dah*	on the left
sağda *sah • dah*	on the right
köşede/köşeyi dönünce *kur • sheh • deh/* *kur • sheh • yee dur • nyun • jeh*	on/around the corner
karşısında *kahr • shih • sihn • dah*	opposite
arkasında *ahr • kah • sihn • dah*	behind
yanında *yah • nihn • dah*	next to
...sonra *...sohn • rah*	after...
kuzey/güney *koo • zay/gyu • nay*	north/south
doğu/batı *doh • oo/bah • tih*	east/west
trafik ışıklarında *trah • feek ih • shihk • lah • rihn • dah*	at the traffic light
kavşakta *kahv • shahk • tah*	at the intersection

PARKING

Can I park here?　　　**Buraya park edebilir miyim?**
boo • rah • yah pahrk eh • deh • bee • leer
mee • yeem

YOU MAY SEE...

	DUR	stop
	YOL VER	yield
	PARK EDİLMEZ	no parking
	GİRİŞ YASAK	no entry
	TEK YÖN	one way
	**YAYA GEÇİDİ**	pedestrian crossing

Where is the nearest parking garage/ parking lot [car park]?	**En yakın park yeri/oto park nerede?** *ehn yah • kihn pahrk yeh • ree/oh • toh pahrk neh • reh • deh*
How much…?	**…ne kadar?** *…neh kah • dahr*
per hour	**Saatlik** *sah • aht • lihk*
per day	**Günlük** *gyun • lyuk*
for overnight	**Bir gecelik** *beer geh • jeh • leek*

BREAKDOWN & REPAIR

My car broke down/ doesn't start.	**Arabam bozuldu/çalışmıyor.** *ah • rah • bahm boh • zool • doo/ chah • lihsh • mih • yohr*
Can you fix it?	**Onarabilir misiniz?** *oh • nah • rah • bee • leer mee • see • neez*
When will it be ready?	**Ne zaman hazır olur?** *neh zah • mahn hah • zihr oh • loor*
How much will it cost?	**Ne kadar para tutar?** *neh kah • dahr pah • rah too • tahr*
I have a puncture/ flat tyre.	**Lastiğim/tekerim patladı.** *lahs • tee • yeem/teh • keh • reem paht • lah • dih*

For Time, see page 23.

ACCIDENTS

There has been an accident.	**Kaza oldu.** *kah • zah ohl • doo*
Call an ambulance/ the police.	**Ambülans/Polis çağırın.** *ahm • byu • lahns/poh • lees chah • ih • rihn*

For Police, see page 146.

PLACES TO STAY

NEED TO KNOW

Can you recommend a hotel?	**Bir otel tavsiye edebilir misiniz?** *beer oh • tehl tahv • see • yeh eh • deh • bee • leer • mee • see • neez*
I have a reservation.	**Yer ayırtmıştım.** *yehr ah • yihrt • mihsh • tihm*
My name is…	**İsmim…** *ees • meem…*
Do you have a room…	**…odanız var mı?** *…oh • dah • nihz vahr mih*
for one/two	**Bir/İki kişilik** *beer/ee • kee kee • shee • leek*
with a bathroom	**Banyolu** *bahn • yoh • loo*
with air conditioning	**Klimalı** *klee • mah • lih*
For tonight.	**Bu gecelik.** *boo geh • jeh • leek*
For two nights.	**İki geceliğine.** *ee • kee geh • jeh • lee • yee • neh*
For one week.	**Bir haftalığına.** *beer hahf • tah • lih • ih • nah*
How much?	**Ne kadar?** *neh kah • dahr*
Do you have anything cheaper?	**Daha ucuz yer var mı?** *dah • hah oo • jooz yehr vahr mih*
When's check-out?	**Saat kaçta otelden ayrılmamız gerekiyor?** *sah • aht kahch • tah oh • tehl • dehn ie • rihl • mah • mihz geh • reh • kee • yohr*

Can I leave this in the safe?	**Bunu kasaya koyabilir miyim?** *boo • <u>noo</u> kah • sah • <u>yah</u> koh • yah • bee • <u>leer</u> mee • yeem*
Can I leave my bags?	**Eşyalarımı bırakabilir miyim?** *ehsh • yah • lah • rih • <u>mih</u> bih • rah • kah • bee • <u>leer</u> mee • yeem*
Can I have the bill/ a receipt?	**Fiş/Hesap alabilir miyim?** *<u>feesh</u>/heh • <u>sahp</u> ah • lah • bee • <u>leer</u> mee • yeem*
I'll pay in cash/by credit card.	**Nakit/Kredi kartı ile ödeyeceğim.** *nah • <u>keet</u>/kreh • <u>dee</u> kahr • <u>tih</u> ee • leh ur • deh • yeh • <u>jeh</u> • yeem*

SOMEWHERE TO STAY

Can you recommend...?	**...tavsiye edebilir misiniz?** *tahv • see • <u>yeh</u> eh • deh • bee • <u>leer</u> mee • see • neez*
a hotel	**bir hotel** *beer oh • <u>tehl</u>*

A range of hotel choices are available in Turkey. In terms of more traditional options, you may choose to stay in **gençlik yurdu** (youth hostels), **pansiyon** (guest houses) or **otel** (hotels). Turkey, however, also offers a number of more special places to stay such as Ottoman mansions, historic houses, Cappadocian cave dwellings, seaside resorts, etc. If you arrive with nowhere booked, contact the **Turizm Danışma Bürosu** (tourist information offices) and they can help you with reservations.

a hostel	**bir pansiyon**
	beer pahn • see • yohn
a campsite	**bir kamp alanı**
	beer kahmp ah • lah • nih
a bed and breakfast	**bir pansiyon**
	beer pahn • see • yohn
What is it near?	**Yakınında ne var?**
	yah • kih • nihn • <u>dah neh</u> vahr
How do I get there?	**Oraya nasıl gidebilirim?**
	oh • rah • yah <u>nah</u> • sihl
	gee • deh • bee • <u>lee</u> • reem

Otel (hotels) in Turkey are labeled with a government-assigned star system (one to five), which generally refers to the number of amenities offered and not how spectacular the hotel may be. Most double rooms are equipped with two twin beds, so if you want a bed for two, be sure to ask. Also, if you want a hotel with air-conditioning, book one that is three-stars or higher. For a more intimate taste of Turkish life, **pansiyon** (guest houses) offer rented rooms and breakfast is usually included in the price. Note that **gençlik yurdu** (youth hostels) are generally only open to card holders.

AT THE HOTEL

I have a reservation.	**Yer ayırtmıştım.**
	yehr ah • yihrt • _mihsh_ • tihm
My name is…	**İsmim…**
	ees • _meem_…
Do you have	**…odanız var mı?**
a room…?	…oh • dah • _nihz_ _vahr_ mih
with a toilet/	**Banyolu/Duşlu**
shower	bahn • yoh • _loo_/doosh • _loo_
with air	**Klimalı**
conditioning	_klee_ • mah • lih
that's smoking/	**Sigara içilen/içilmeyen**
non-smoking	see • _gah_ • rah ee • chee • _lehn_/
	ee • _cheel_ • meh • yehn
For tonight.	**Bu gecelik.**
	boo geh • jeh • _leek_
For two nights.	**İki geceliğine.**
	ee • _kee_ geh • jeh • lee • yee • _neh_
For one week.	**Bir haftalığına.**
	beer hahf • tah • lih • gih • _nah_
Does the hotel	**Otelde bir…var mı?**
have…?	oh • _tehl_ • deh beer…_vahr_ mih

a computer	**bilgisayar**
	beel • gee • sah • <u>yahr</u>
an elevator [a lift]	**asansör**
	ah • sahn • <u>surr</u>
(wireless) internet service	**(kablosuz) internet hizmeti**
	(kahb • loh • <u>sooz</u>) een • tehr • <u>neht</u> heez • meh • <u>tee</u>
room service	**oda servisi**
	oh • <u>dah</u> sehr • vee • <u>see</u>
a pool	**havuzu**
	hah • voo • zoo
a gym	**jimnastik**
	jeem • nahs • <u>teek</u>
I need…	**Bana bir…lâzım.**
	bah • <u>nah</u> beer…liah • zihm
an extra bed	**ek yatak**
	ehk yah • <u>tahk</u>
a cot	**bebek yatağı**
	beh • <u>behk</u> yah • tah • <u>gih</u>
a crib	**çocuk yatağı**
	choh • <u>jook</u> yah • tah • <u>gih</u>

YOU MAY HEAR…

Lütfen pasaportunuz/kredi kartınız.
<u>lyut</u> • fehn pas • sah • por • too • <u>nooz</u>/ kreh • <u>dee</u> kahr • tih • <u>nihz</u>

Your passport/ credit card, please.

Bu formu doldurun lütfen.
<u>boo</u> fohr • moo dohl • <u>doo</u> • roon <u>lyut</u> • fehn

Please fill out this form.

Burasını imzalayın lütfen.
<u>boo</u> • rah • sih • <u>nih</u> eem • zah • <u>lah</u> • yihn <u>lyut</u> • fehn

Please sign here.

PRICE

How much per night/ week?	**Geceliği/Haftalığı ne kadar?** *geh • jeh • lee • <u>yee</u>/ hahf • tah • lih • <u>ih</u> neh kah • dahr*
Does the price include breakfast/ sales tax [VAT]?	**Fiyata kahvaltı/KDV dahil mi?** *fee • yah • <u>tah</u> kah • vahl • <u>tih</u>/ kah • deh • <u>veh</u> dah • <u>heel</u> mee*

PREFERENCES

Can I see the room?	**Odayı görebilir miyim?** *oh • die • yih gur • reh • bee • leer mee • yeem*
I'd like a...room.	**... bir oda istiyorum** *...beer oh • dah ees • tee • yoh • room*
better	**Daha iyi** *dah • hah ee • yih*
bigger	**Daha büyük** *dah • hah byu • yuhk*
cheaper	**Daha ucuz** *dah • hah oo • jooz*
quieter	**Daha sessiz** *dah • hah sehs • seez*
I'll take it.	**Alıyorum.** *ah • lih • yoh • room*
No, I won't take it.	**Almıyorum.** *ahl • mih • yoh • room*

QUESTIONS

Where's...?	**...nerede?** *...<u>neh</u> • reh • deh*

the bar	**Bar**	
	bahr	
the bathrooms	**Tuvalet**	
	too • vah • leht	
the elevator [lift]	**Asansör**	
	ah • sahn • surr	
Can I have...?	**...alabilir miyim?**	
	...ah • lah • bee • leer mee • yeem	
a blanket	**Battaniye**	
	baht • tah • nee • yeh	
an iron	**Ütü**	
	yu • tyu	
a pillow	**Yastık**	
	yahs • tihk	
soap	**Sabun**	
	sah • boon	
toilet paper	**Tuvalet kağıdı**	
	too • vah • leht kah • ih • dih	
a towel	**Havlu**	
	hahv • loo	

i

Turkish electricity is generally 220 volts, though 110 volts may be found in the European part of Istanbul. British and American appliances will need an adapter.

Do you have an adapter for this?	**Bunun için bir adaptörünüz var mı?**
	boo • <u>noon</u> ee • cheen beer
	ah • dahp • tur • ryu • <u>nyuz</u> <u>vahr</u> mih
How do I turn on the lights?	**Işıkları nasıl açabilirim?**
	ih • shihk • lah • <u>rih</u> <u>nah</u> • sihl
	ah • chah • bee • <u>lee</u> • reem
Could you wake me at...?	**Beni saat...oyandırabilir misiniz?**
	beh • <u>nee</u> sah • <u>aht</u>...
	oh • yahn • dih • rah • bee • <u>leer</u>
	mee • see • neez
Can I leave this in the safe?	**Bunu kasada bırakabilir miyim?**
	boo • noo kah • sah • dah
	bih • rah • kah • bee • leer mee • yeem?
Could I have my things from the safe?	**Kasadan eşyalarımı alabilir miyim?**
	kah • sah • <u>dahn</u> ehsh • <u>yah</u> • lah • rih • mih
	ah • lah • bee • <u>leer</u> mee • yeem
Is there mail/ a message for me?	**Benim için posta/mesaj var mı?**
	beh • <u>neem</u> ee • cheen pohs • <u>tah</u>/
	meh • <u>sahj</u> <u>vahr</u> mih
Do you have a laundry service?	**Çamaşırhane hizmetiniz var mı?**
	chah • mah • shihr • hah • neh
	heez • meh • tee • neez vahr mih

👁

YOU MAY SEE...

İTİNİZ/ÇEKİNİZ	push/pull
TUVALET	restroom [toilet]
DUŞ	shower
ASANSÖR	elevator [lift]
MERDİVENLER	stairs
ÇAMAŞIRHANE	laundry
RAHATSIZ ETMEYİNİZ	do not disturb
YANGIN KAPISI	fire door
ACİL ÇIKIŞ	emergency exit
ARAMA-UYANDIRMA	wake-up call

PROBLEMS

There's a problem. **Bir sorun var.**
beer soh • <u>roon</u> vahr

I've lost my key/key card. **Anahtarımı/Anahtar kartımı kaybettim.**
ah • nah • tah • rih • <u>mih</u>/ah • nah • <u>tahr</u> kahr • tih • <u>mih</u> kie • beht • teem

I've locked myself out of my room. **Kapıda kaldım.**
kah • pih • <u>dah</u> kahl • <u>dihm</u>

There's no hot water/toilet paper. **Sıcak su/Tuvalet kağıdı yok.**
sih • <u>jahk</u> soo/ too • vah • <u>leht</u> kah • ih • <u>dih</u> yok

The room is dirty. **Oda kirli.**
oh • <u>dah</u> keer • leeh

There are bugs in our room. **Odamızda böcek var.**
oh • dah • mihz • <u>dah</u> bur • <u>jehk</u> vahr

Can you fix…? **…tamir edebilir misiniz?**
…tah • meer eh • deh • bee • leer
mee • see • neez

the air **Klimayı**
conditioning *klee • mah • yih*

the fan **Vantilatörü**
vahn • tee • lah • tur • ryu

the heat [heating] **Isıtıcıyı**
ih • sih • tih • jih • yih

the light **Işığı**
ih • shih • ih

the TV **Televizyonu**
teh • leh • vee • zyoh • noo

the toilet **Tuvaleti**
too • vah • leh • tee

…has broken down. **…kırık.**
…kih • rihk

I'd like to move to **Başka bir odaya taşınmak istiyorum.**
another room. *bahsh • kah beer oh • dah • yah*
tah • shihn • mahk ees • tee • yoh • room

ⓘ

Tipping in hotels is not necessary, but you may offer
a few Lira to porters or to attentive staff for their help.

CHECKING OUT

When's check-out? **Saat kaçta otelden ayrılmamız**
gerekiyor?
sah • aht kahch • tah oh • tehl • dehn
ie • rihl • mah • mihz geh • reh • kee • yohr

Could I leave my **Çantalarımı buraya…bırakabilir miyim?**
bags here until…? *chan • tah • lah • rih • mih boo • rah • yah…*
bih • rah • kah • bee • leer mee • yeem

Can I have an itemized bill/ a receipt?	**Dökümlü hesap/Fiş alabilir miyim?**
	dur • kyum • lyu heh • sahp/ feesh ah • lah • bee • leer mee • yeem
I think there's a mistake in this bill.	**Sanırım bu hesapta bir yanlışlık var.**
	sah • nih • rihm boo heh • sahp • tah beer yan • lihsh • lihk vahr
I'll pay in cash/by credit card.	**Nakit/Kredi kartı ile ödeyeceğim.**
	nah • keet/kreh • dee kahr • tih ee • leh ur • deh • yeh • jeh • yeem

RENTING

I've reserved an apartment/a room.	**Bir apartman/oda tuttum.**
	beer ah • pahrt • mahn/ oh • dah toot • toom
My name is…	**İsmim…**
	ees • meem…
Can I have the key/ key card?	**Anahtarı/Anahtar kartını alabilir miyim?**
	ah • nah • tah • rih/ah • nah • tahr kahr • tih • nih ah • lah • bee • leer mee • yeem
Are there…?	**…var mı?**
	…vahr mih
dishes	**Tabak çanak**
	tah • bahk chah • nahk

pillows	**Yastık**	
	yahs • tihk	
sheets	**Çarşaf**	
	chahr • shahf	
towels	**Havlu**	
	hahv • loo	
When/Where do I put out the bins?	**Çöpü ne zaman/nereye çıkarayım?**	
	chur • pyu neh zah • mahn/	
	neh • reh • yeh chih • kah • rah • yihm	
...is broken.	**...bozuldu.**	
	...boh • zool • doo	
How does...work?	**...nasıl çalışıyor?**	
	...nah • sihl chah • lih • shih • yohr	
the air conditioner	**Klima**	
	klee • mah	
the dishwasher	**Bulaşık makinesi**	
	boo • lah • shihk mah • kee • neh • see	
the freezer	**Dondurucu**	
	dohn • doo • roo • joo	
the heater	**Isıtıcı**	
	ih • sih • tih • jih	
the microwave	**Mikrodalga**	
	meek • roh • dahl • gah	
the refrigerator	**Buzdolabı**	
	booz • doh • lah • bih	

the stove	**Fırın**
	fih • rihn
the washing machine	**Çamaşır makinesi**
	chah • mah • shihr mah • kee • neh • see

DOMESTIC ITEMS

I need...	**...ihtiyacım var.**
	...eeh • tee • yah • jihm vahr
an adapter	**Adaptöre**
	ah • dahp • tur • reh
aluminum [kitchen] foil	**Alimünyum kağıdına**
	ah • lee • myu • nyoom kah • ih • dih • nah
a bottle opener	**Şişe açacağına**
	shee • sheh ah • chah • jah • ih • nah
a broom	**Süpürgeye**
	syu • pyur • geh • yeh
a can opener	**Konserve açacağına**
	kohn • sehr • veh ah • chah • jah • ih • nah
cleaning supplies	**Temizlik maddelerine**
	teh • meez • leek mahd • deh • leh • ree • neh
a corkscrew	**Şarap açacağına**
	shah • rahp ah • chah • jah • ih • nah
detergent	**Deterjana**
	deh • tehr • jah • nah
dishwashing liquid	**Bulaşık deterjanına**
	boo • lah • shihk deh • tehr • jah • nih • nah
garbage [rubbish] bags	**Çöp torbalarına**
	churp tohr • bah • lah • rih • nah
a light bulb	**Ampula**
	ahm • poo • lah
matches	**Kibrite**
	keeb • ree • teh

a mop	**Yer bezine**
	yehr beh • zee • <u>neh</u>
napkins	**Kağıt peçeteye**
	kah • <u>iht</u> peh • <u>cheh</u> • teh • yeh
paper towels	**Kağıt havluya**
	kah • <u>iht</u> hahv • loo • <u>yah</u>
plastic wrap	**Plastik ambalaj kağıdına**
[cling film]	*plahs • <u>teek</u> ahm • bah • <u>lahj</u>*
	kah • ih • dih • <u>nah</u>
a plunger	**Plançere**
	<u>plahn</u> • cheh • reh
scissors	**Makasa**
	mah • kah • <u>sah</u>
a vacuum cleaner	**Elektrikli süpürgeye**
	eh • lehk • treek • <u>lee</u> syu • pyur • geh • <u>yeh</u>

For In the Kitchen, see page 194.

AT THE HOSTEL

Do you have any places left for tonight?	**Bu gece için yer var mı?**
	boo geh • <u>jeh</u> ee • cheen
	yehr <u>vahr</u> mih
Can I have...?	**...alabilir miyim?**
	...ah • lah • bee • <u>leer</u> mee • yeem

a single/double room	**tek kişilik/cift kişilik oda**
	tehk kee•shee•leek/
	cheeft kee•shee•leek oh•dah
a blanket	**Battaniye**
	baht•tah•nee•<u>yeh</u>
a pillow	**Yastık**
	yahs•<u>tihk</u>
sheets	**Çarşaf**
	chahr•<u>shahf</u>
towels	**Havlu**
	hahv•<u>loo</u>
What time do you lock up?	**Kapılar saat kaçta kapanıyor?**
	kah•pih•<u>lahr</u> sah•<u>aht</u> kahch•<u>tah</u>
	kah•pah•nih•yohr
Do I need a membership card?	**Üyelik kartına ihtiyacım var mı?**
	yu•yeh•leek kahr•tih•nah
	eeh•tee•yah•jihm vahr mih?
Here's my international student card.	**Buyrun uluslararası öğrenci kartım.**
	booy•roon oo•loos•lahr•ah•rah•sih
	ur•rehn•jee kahr•tihm

> Hostels are located throughout Turkey and are a good option for those traveling through Turkey on a restricted budget. Keep in mind, though, that you usually need to be a card-holder in order to stay in a hostel here. ⓘ

GOING CAMPING

Can I camp here?	**Burada kamp yapabilir miyim?**
	<u>boo</u>•rah•dah kahmp
	yah•pah•bee•<u>leer</u> mee•yeem
Is there a campsite near here?	**Yakınlarda bir kamp alanı var mı?**
	yah•<u>kihn</u>•lahr•<u>dah</u> beer kahmp
	ah•lah•nih <u>vahr</u> mih

What is the charge per day/week?	**Günlüğü/Haftalığı ne kadar?**
	gyun • lyu • yu/hahf • tah • lih • ih neh kah • dahr
Are there…?	**…var mı?**
	…vahr mih
cooking facilities	**Pişirme olanakları**
	pee • sheer • meh oh • lah • nahk • lah • rih
electric outlets	**Elektrik prizi**
	eh • lehk • treek pree • zee
laundry facilities	**Çamaşırhane**
	chah • mah • shihr • hah • neh
showers	**Duş**
	doosh
tents for hire	**Kiralık çadırlar**
	kee • rah • lihk chah • dihr • lahr
Where can I empty the chemical toilet?	**Portatif tuvaleti nereye dökebilirim?**
	pohr • tah • teef too • vah • leh • tee neh • reh • yeh dur • keh • bee • lee • reem

For In the Kitchen, see page 194.

YOU MAY SEE…

İÇME SUYU	drinking water
KAMP YAPMAK YASAKTIR	no camping
ATEŞ/MANGAL YAKMAK YASAKTIR	no fires/barbecues

COMMUNICATIONS

NEED TO KNOW

Where's an internet cafe?	**İnternet kafe nerede?** *een • tehr • <u>neht</u> kah • <u>feh</u> eh • reh • deh*
Can I access the internet/check e-mail here?	**Burada internete girebilir/ postalarımı kontrol edebilir miyim?** *<u>boo</u> • rah • dah een • tehr • neh • <u>teh</u> gee • reh • bee • <u>leer</u>/ pohs • tah • lah • rih • <u>mih</u> kohn • <u>trohl</u> eh • deh • bee • <u>leer</u> mee • yeem*
How much per hour/half hour?	**Saati/Yarım saati ne kadar?** *sah • ah • <u>tee</u>/yah • rihm sah • ah • <u>tee</u> neh kah • dahr*
How do I connect/ log on?	**Nasıl bağlanabilirim/girebilirim?** *<u>nah</u> • sihl bah • lah • nah • bee • <u>lee</u> • reem/ gee • reh • bee • <u>lee</u> • reem*
I'd like a phone card, please.	**Bir telefon kartı lütfen.** *beer teh • leh • <u>fohn</u> kahr • <u>tih</u> <u>lyut</u> • fehn*
Can I have your phone number?	**Telefon numaranızı öğrenebilir miyim?** *teh • leh • <u>fohn</u> noo • <u>mah</u> • rah • nih • zih ur • reh • neh • bee • <u>leer</u> mee • yeem*
Here's my number/ e-mail address.	**İşte numaram/e-posta adresim.** *eesh • teh noo • <u>mah</u> • rahm/ eh • pohs • <u>tah</u> ahd • reh • seem*
Call me.	**Beni arayın.** *beh • <u>nee</u> ah • <u>rah</u> • yihn*
E-mail me.	**Bana yazın.** *bah • <u>nah</u> <u>yah</u> • zihn*

Hello, this is…	**Merhaba, ben…**
	mehr • hah • bah behn…
I'd like to speak to…	**…ile konuşmak istiyorum.**
	…ee • leh koh • noosh • mahk ees • tee • yoh • room
Can you repeat that, please?	**Tekrar eder misiniz lütfen?**
	tehk • rahr eh • dehr mee • see • neez lyut • fehn
I'll call back later.	**Daha sonra arayacağım.**
	dah • hah sohn • rah ah • rah • yah • jah • ihm
Goodbye. (said by first person)	**Hoşçakalın.**
	hosh • chah • kah • lihn
Goodbye. (said by the other person)	**Güle güle.**
	gyu • leh gyu • leh
Where is the post office?	**Postane nerede?**
	pohs • tah • neh neh • reh • deh
I'd like to send this to…	**Bunu…göndermek istiyorum.**
	boo • noo… gurn • dehr • mehk ees • tee • yoh • room

ONLINE

Where's an internet cafe?	**İnternet kafe nerede?**
	een • tehr • neht kah • feh neh • reh • deh
Does it have wireless internet?	**Kablosuz internet var mı?**
	kahb • loh • sooz een • tehr • neht vahr mih
What is the WiFi password?	**Kablosuz ağın şifresi nedir?**
	kahb • loh • sooz ah • ihn sheef • reh • see neh • deer
Is the WiFi free?	**Kablosuz ağ ücretsiz mi?**
	kahb • loh • sooz ah yuch • reht • seez mee

Do you have bluetooth?	**Bluetooth var mı?**
	Bluetooth vahr mih
How do I turn the computer on/off?	**Bilgisayarı nasıl açabilirim/ kapatabilirim?**
	beel • gee • sah • yah • <u>rih</u> <u>nah</u> • sihl ah • chah • bee • <u>lee</u> • reem/ kah • pah • tah • bee • <u>lee</u> • reem
Can I...?	**...bilir miyim?**
	...bee • <u>leer</u> mee • yeem
access the internet here	**Buradan internete bağlana**
	<u>boo</u> • rah • dahn een • tehr • neh • <u>teh</u> bah • lah • nah
check e-mail	**E-postaya baka**
	eh • poh • stah • <u>yah</u> bah • <u>kah</u>
print	**Basa**
	bah • <u>sah</u>
plug in/charge my laptop/iPhone/ iPad/BlackBerry?	**Diz üstü bilgisayarımı/iPhone'umu/ iPad'imi fişe takabilir miyim/şarj edebilir miyim?**
	deez yus • tyu beel • gee • sah • yah • rih • mi/ iPhone'um • hu/iPad'im • hi feesh • eh tah • kah • bee • leer mee • yeem/sharj eh • deh • bee • leer mee • yeem

access Skype?	**Skype'ı kullanabilir miyim?**
	Skype'ih kool • lah • nah • bee • leer
	mee • yeem
How much per hour/	**Saati/Yarım saati ne kadar?**
half hour?	*sah • ah • tee/yah • rihm*
	sah • ah • tee neh kah • dahr
How do I...?	**Nasıl...?**
	nah • sihl...
connect/	**bağlanırım/bağlantıyı keserim**
disconnect	*bagh • lah • nih • rihm/*
	bah • lahn • tih • yih keh • seh • reem
log on/off	**giriş/çıkış yaparım**
	gee • reesh/chih • kihsh yah • pah • rihm
type this symbol	**bu sembolü yazarım**
	boo sehm • boh • lyu yah • zah • rehm
What's your e-mail?	**E-posta adresiniz nedir?**
	eh • pohs • tah ahd • reh • see • neez
	neh • deer
My e-mail is...	**E-posta adresim...**
	eh • pohs • tah ahd • reh • seem...

YOU MAY SEE...

KAPAT	close
SİL	delete
E-POSTA	e-mail
ÇIKIŞ	logout
YARDIM	help
ANINDA MUHABBET	instant messenger
İNTERNET	internet
GİRİŞ	login
YENİ MESAJ	new message
AÇ/KAPA	on/off
AÇIK	open
YAZDIR	print
KAYDET	save
GÖNDER	send
KULLANICI İSMİ/ŞİFRE	username/password
KABLOSUZ İNTERNET	wireless internet

SOCIAL MEDIA

Are you on Facebook/ Twitter?	**Facebook/Twitter'da mısın?** *Facebook/Twitter'dah mih • sihn*
What's your user name?	**Kullanıcı adın ne?** *kool • lah • nih • jih ah • dihn neh*
I'll add you as a friend.	**Seni arkadaş olarak ekleyeceğim.** *seh • nee ahr • kah • dash oh • lah • rahk ehk • leh • yeh • jeh • yeem*
I'll follow you on Twitter.	**Seni Twitter'da takip edeceğim.** *seh • nee Twitter'dah tah • keep eh • deh • jeh • yeem*
Are you following...?	**... takip ediyor musun?** *...tah • keep eh • dee • yohr moo • soon*

I'll put the pictures on Facebook/Twitter. **Resimleri Facebook/Twitter'a koyacağım.**

reh • seem • leh • ree Facebook/Tweeter'ah koh • yah • jah • yihm

I'll tag you in the pictures. **Seni resimlerde etiketleyeceğim.**

seh • nee reh • seem • lehr • deh eh • tee • keht • lih • yeh • jeh • yeem

PHONE

A phone card/prepaid phone, please. **Bir telefon kartı/kontörlü telefon lütfen.**

beer teh • leh • <u>fohn</u> kahr • <u>tih</u>/ kohn • tyur • <u>lyu</u> teh • leh • <u>fohn</u> <u>lyut</u> • fehn

How much? **Ne kadar?**

<u>neh</u> kah • dahr

My phone doesn't work here. **Telefonum burda çalışmıyor.**

teh • leh • foh • <u>noom</u> boor • <u>dah</u> chah • <u>lihsh</u> • mih • yohr

What's the area/country code for...? **...için bölge/ülke kodu nedir?**

...ee • <u>cheen</u> burl • <u>geh</u>/ yul • <u>keh</u> koh • doo <u>neh</u> • deer

What's the number for Information? **Bilinmeyen numaralar kaç?**

bee • <u>leen</u> • meh • yehn noo • <u>mah</u> • rah • lahr <u>kahch</u>

YOU MAY HEAR...

Kim arıyor?
keem ah • rih • yohr

Who's calling?

Bir dakika lütfen.
beer dah • kee • kah lyut • fehn

Hold on, please.

Telefona gelemez.
teh • leh • foh • nah geh • leh • mehz

He/She can't come to the phone.

Mesaj bırakmak istiyor musunuz?
meh • sahj bih • rahk • mahk ees • tee • yohr moo • soo • nooz

Would you like to leave a message?

Daha sonra/On dakika içinde arayın.
dah • hah sohn • rah/ ohn dah • kee • kah ee • cheen • deh ah • rah • yihn

Call back later/ in 10 minutes.

Sizi tekrar arayabilir mi?
see • zee tehk • rahr ah • rah • yah • bee • leer mee

Can he/she call you back?

Telefon numaranızı öğrenebilir miyim?
teh • leh • fohn noo • mah • rah • nih • zih ur • reh • neh • bee • leer mee • yeem

What's your number?

I'd like the number for...

...için numarayı istiyorum.
...ee • cheen noo • mah • rah • yih ees • tee • yoh • room

Can I have your number?

Telefon numaranızı öğrenebilir miyim?
teh • leh • fohn noo • mah • rah • nih • zih ur • reh • neh • bee • leer mee • yeem

Here's my number.

İşte numaram.
eesh • teh noo • mah • rahm

Please call me.

Lütfen beni arayın.
lyut • fehn beh • nee ah • rah • yihn

Please text me.	**Lütfen bana yazın.**
	lyut • fehn bah • _nah yah_ • zihn
I'll call you.	**Sizi arayacağım.**
	see • _zee_ ah • rah • yah • _jah_ • yihm
I'll text you.	**Size yazarım.**
	see • _zeh_ yah • _zah_ • rihm

For Numbers, see page 20.

TELEPHONE ETIQUETTE

Hello, this is...	**Merhaba, ben...**
	mehr • hah • bah _behn_...
I'd like to speak to...	**...ile konuşmak istiyorum.**
	...ee • _leh_ koh • noosh • _mahk_
	ees • _tee_ • yoh • room
Extension...	**Dahili hattı...**
	dah • _hee_ • lee haht • _tih_...
Can you speak louder/more slowly, please?	**Daha yüksek/yavaş sesle konuşur musunuz lütfen?**
	dah • _hah_ yuk • _sehk_/yah • _vahsh_
	sehs • leh koh • noo • _shoor_
	moo • soo • nooz _lyut_ • fehn

Can you repeat that, please?	**Tekrar eder misiniz lütfen?**
	tehk • rahr eh • dehr
	mee • see • neez lyut • fehn
I'll call back later.	**Daha sonra tekrar ararım.**
	dah • hah sohn • rah
	tehk • rahr ah • rah • rihm
Goodbye. (said by first person)	**Hoşçakalın.**
	hosh • chah • kah • lihn
Goodbye. (said by second person)	**Güle güle.**
	gyu • leh gyu • leh

FAX

Can I send/receive a fax here?	**Buradan faks gönderebilir/alabilir miyim?**
	boo • rah • dahn fahks
	gurn • deh • reh • bee • leer/
	ah • lah • bee • leer mee • yeem
What's the fax number?	**Faks numarası kaç?**
	fahks noo • mah • rah • sih kahch
Please fax this to…	**Lütfen bunu…fakslayın.**
	lyut • fehn boo • noo…fahks • lah • yihn

POST

Where's the post office/mailbox [postbox]?	**Postahane/Posta kutusu nerede?**
	pohs • tah • neh/pohs • tah
	koo • too • soo neh • reh • deh
A stamp for this postcard/letter, please.	**Bu kartpostal/mektup için pul lütfen.**
	boo kahrt • pohs • tahl/mehk • toop
	ee • cheen pool lyut • fehn
How much?	**Ne kadar?**
	neh kah • dahr

I want to send this package by airmail/express.	**Bu paketi uçak/özel ulak ile göndermek istiyorum.**
	boo pah • keh • <u>tee</u> oo • <u>chahk</u>/ur • <u>zehl</u> oo • <u>lahk</u> ee • leh gurn • dehr • <u>mehk</u> ees • <u>tee</u> • yoh • room
A receipt, please.	**Lütfen bir fiş verin.**
	<u>lyut</u> • fehn beer feesh <u>veh</u> • reen

YOU MAY HEAR...

Lütfen gümrük beyanını doldurunuz.
<u>lyut</u> • fehn gyum • <u>ryuk</u> beh • yah • nih • <u>nih</u> dohl • <u>doo</u> • roo • nooz

Değeri nedir?
deh • yeh • <u>ree neh</u> • deer

İçinde ne var?
ee • cheen • <u>deh neh</u> vahr

Please fill out the customs declaration form.
What's the value?
What's inside?

Post offices in Turkey display a yellow sign with
the letters **PTT (Posta Telegraf Telefon)** (Post Telegraph
Telephone) in blue. Aside from sending letters or packages,
you can also change money, make phone calls or buy phone
cards. Major post offices in more touristy areas may stay
open until midnight, with a more restricted schedule on
Sunday. Smaller post offices are generally only open until
5:00 p.m.

SIGHTSEEING

NEED TO KNOW

Where's the tourist office?	**Turist danışma bürosu nerede?** too • _reest_ dah • nihsh • _mah_ byu • roh • soo _neh_ • reh • deh
What are the main points of interest?	**Başlıca ilginç yerler nelerdir?** bahsh • _lih_ • jah eel • geench yehr • _lehr_ neh • _lehr_ • deer
Do you have tours in English?	**İngilizce turlarınız var mı?** een • geh • _leez_ • jeh toor • lah • rih • _nihz_ _vahr_ mih
Can I have a map/ guide?	**Harita/Rehber alabilir miyim?** hah • _ree_ • tah/reh • _ber_ ah • lah • bee • _leer_ mee • yeem

TOURIST INFORMATION

Do you have any information on...?	**...hakkında bir bilginiz var mı?**
	...hahk • kihn • dah beer beel • gee • neez vahr mih
Can you recommend...?	**...önerebilir misiniz?**
	...ur • neh • reh • bee • leer mee • see • neez
a boat trip	**Bir gemi gezisi**
	beer geh • mee geh • zee • see
an excursion	**Bir gezinti**
	beer geh • zeen • tee
a sightseeing tour	**Bir tur**
	beer toor

For Asking Directions, see page 65.

ⓘ

Turizm Danışma Bürosu (tourist information offices) are located in cities throughout Turkey. In smaller cities, the office is often located in or near the main square. Big cities usually have several offices. The tourist office can provide maps and information about the area and help in making reservations. Travel agents are also helpful in assisting with information and can often offer good rates on hotel reservations.

ON TOUR

I'd like to go on the tour to...	**...turla gitmek istiyorum.**
	...toor • lah geet • mehk ees • tee • yoh • room

When's the next tour?	**Bir sonraki tur ne zaman?**
	beer <u>sohn</u> • rah • kee toor <u>neh</u> zah • mahn
Are there tours in English?	**İngilizce turlar var mı?**
	een • gee • <u>leez</u> • jeh toor • <u>lahr</u> <u>vahr</u> mih
Is there an English-speaking guide?	**İngilizce konuşan bir rehber var mı?**
	een • gee • <u>leez</u> • jeh koh • noo • <u>shahn</u> beer reh • <u>behr</u> <u>vahr</u> mih
What time do we leave/return?	**Saat kaçta ayrılacağız/döneceğiz?**
	sah • <u>aht</u> kahch • <u>tah</u> ie • rih • lah • <u>jah</u> • ihz/ dur • neh • <u>jeh</u> • eez
We'd like to have a look at the…	**…bakmak istiyoruz.**
	…bahk • <u>mahk</u> ees • <u>tee</u> • yoh • rooz
Can we stop here…?	**Burada…durabilir miyiz?**
	<u>boo</u> • rah • dah…doo • rah • bee • <u>leer</u> mee • yeez
to take photographs	**fotoğraf çekmek için**
	foh • toh • <u>rahf</u> chehk • <u>mehk</u> ee • cheen
for souvenirs	**hediyelik eşya satın almak için**
	heh • dee • yeh • <u>leek</u> ehsh • <u>yah</u> sah • <u>tihn</u> ahl • <u>mahk</u> ee • cheen
to use the restroom [toilet]	**tuvalete gitmek için**
	too • vah • leh • <u>teh</u> geet • <u>mehk</u> ee • <u>cheen</u>

Is there access for the disabled?	**Özürlüler girebilir mi?** *ur • zyur • lyu • <u>lehr</u>* *gee • reh • bee • <u>leer</u> mee*

For Tickets, see page 45.

SEEING THE SIGHTS

Where is...?	**...nerede?** ... *<u>neh</u> • reh • deh*
the battleground	**Muharebe meydanı** *moo • hah • reh • <u>beh</u> may • dah • nih*
the botanical garden	**Botanik bahçesi** *boh • tah • <u>neek</u> bah • cheh • <u>see</u>*
the castle	**Kale** *kah • <u>leh</u>*
the downtown area	**Kent merkezi** *kehnt mehr • keh • <u>zee</u>*
the fountain	**Çeşme** *chehsh • <u>meh</u>*
the library	**Kütüphane** *kyu • tyup • hah • <u>neh</u>*
the market	**Pazar** *pah • <u>zahr</u>*

the museum	**Müze**
	myu • <u>zeh</u>
the old town	**Eski kent**
	ehs • <u>kee</u> kehnt
the palace	**Saray**
	sah • <u>rie</u>
the park	**Park**
	pahrk
the shopping area	**Alış veriş merkezi**
	ah • <u>lihsh</u> veh • <u>reesh</u> mehr • keh • <u>zee</u>
the town square	**Kasaba meydanı**
	kah • sah • <u>bah</u> may • dah • <u>nih</u>
Can you show me on the map?	**Bana haritada gösterebilir misiniz?**
	bah • <u>nah</u> hah • <u>ree</u> • tah • dah gurs • teh • reh • bee • <u>leer</u> mee • see • neez
It's...	**...-dir.**
	...deer
amazing	**Hayret verici**
	hie • <u>reht</u> veh • ree • <u>jee</u>
beautiful	**Güzel**
	gyu • <u>zehl</u>
boring	**Sıkıcı**
	sih • kih • <u>jih</u>

interesting	**İlginç**
	eel • <u>ginch</u>
magnificent	**Muhteşem**
	mooh • teh • <u>shehm</u>
romantic	**Romantik**
	roh • mahn • <u>teek</u>
strange	**Şaşırtıcı**
	shah • shihr • tih • <u>jih</u>
stunning	**Çarpıcı**
	chahr • pih • <u>jih</u>
terrible	**Berbat**
	behr • <u>baht</u>
ugly	**Çirkin**
	cheer • <u>keen</u>
I like it.	**Beğendim.**
	beh • yehn • <u>deem</u>
I don't like it.	**Beğenmedim.**
	beh • <u>yehn</u> • meh • deem

RELIGIOUS SITES

Where's...?	**...nerede?**
	...<u>neh</u> • reh • deh

the cathedral	**Katedral**
	kah • tehd • rahl
the Catholic/ Protestant church	**Katolik/Protestan kilisesi**
	kah • toh • leek/ proh • tehs • tahn kee • lee • seh • see
the mosque	**Cami**
	jah • mee
the shrine	**Mabet**
	mah • baht
the synagogue	**Havra**
	hahv • rah
the temple	**Tapınak**
	tah • pih • nahk
What time is mass/ the service?	**Ayin/İbadet saat kaçta?**
	ah • yihn/ee • bah • deht sah • aht kahch • tah

ⓘ

Turkey is a Muslim country and the majority of the population belongs to the Sunni branch of Islam. It is, however, a secular state. Individuals are guaranteed freedom of religion by the constitution, which at the same time protects religious groups. The constitution also specifies that the political system must be explicitly religion-free. That means religious groups may not form political parties or establish schools based on a particular faith. Turkey also prohibits wearing religious garments, such as head covers, in all government buildings as well as schools and universities.

ACTIVITIES

SHOPPING	104
SPORT & LEISURE	127
TRAVELING WITH CHILDREN	137

SHOPPING

NEED TO KNOW

Where is the market/mall [shopping centre]?	**Market/Alış veriş merkezi nerede?** _mahr • keht/ah • lihsh_ veh • _reesh_ _mehr • keh • zee neh • reh • deh_
I'm just looking.	**Sadece bakıyorum.** _sah • deh • jeh_ bah • _kih • yoh • room_
Can you help me?	**Bana yardım edebilir misiniz?** _bah • nah yahr • dihm_ _eh • deh • bee • leer_ mee • see • neez_
I'm being helped.	**Yardım alıyorum.** _yahr • dihm ah • lih • yoh • room_
How much?	**Ne kadar?** _neh_ kah • dahr
That one.	**Şunu.** _shoo • noo_
That's all, thanks.	**Hepsi bu, teşekkürler.** _hehp • see_ boo teh • shehk • kyur • _lehr_
Where do I pay?	**Nereye ödeyeceğim?** _neh • reh • yeh_ ur • _deh • yeh • jeh • yeem_
I'll pay in cash/by credit card.	**Nakit/Kredi kartı ile ödeyeceğim.** nah • _keet/kreh • dee kahr • tih ee • leh_ ur • _deh • yeh • jeh • yeem_
A receipt, please.	**Fatura lütfen.** _fah • too • rah lyut • fehn_

ⓘ

One thing not to miss while in Turkey is the weekly
pazar (neighborhood market), found outside in almost every
town throughout the country. In Istanbul, be sure to visit the
Kapali Çarşı (Covered market or Grand Bazaar), the **Mısır
Çarşısı** (Spice Market) and the **Balık Pazarı** (Fish Bazaar).
Beware of pickpockets though. They are prevalent in these
places, so tourists should pay attention their valuables.

AT THE SHOPS

Where is…?	**…nerede?** …
	neh • reh • deh
the antique store	**Antikacı**
	ahn • tee • kah • jih
the bakery	**Fırın**
	fih • rihn
the bank	**Banka**
	bahn • kah
the bookstore	**Kitapçı**
	kee • tahp • chih
the clothing store	**Elbise mağazası**
	ehl • bee • seh mah • ah • zah • sih
the delicatessen	**Şarküteri**
	shahr • kyu • teh • ree
the department store	**Mağaza**
	mah • ah • zah
the gift shop	**Hediyelik eşya dükkanı**
	heh • dee • yeh • leek ehsh • yah dyuk • kah • nih
the health food store	**Sağlıklı yiyecekler dükkanı**
	sah • lihk • lih yee • yeh • jehk • lehr dyuk • kah • nih

YOU MAY HEAR...

Yardımcı olabilir miyim?
*yahr • dihm • jih oh • lah • bee • leer
mee • yeem*

Can I help you?

Bir dakika.
beer dah • kee • kah

One moment.

Ne istersiniz?
neh ees • tehr • see • neez

What would you like?

Başka bir şey?
bahsh • kah beer shay

Anything else?

the jeweler	**Kuyumcu**	
	koo • yoom • joo	
the liquor store	**Tekel bayii**	
	teh • kehl bah • yee • ee	
the market	**Market**	
	mahr • keht	
the pastry shop	**Pastane**	
	pahs • tah • neh	
the pharmacy [chemist]	**Eczane**	
	ehj • zah • neh	

the produce [grocery] store	**Manav**
	mah • nahv
the shoe store	**Ayakkabıcı**
	ah • yahk • kah • bih • jih
the shopping mall [centre]	**Alış veriş merkezi**
	ah • lihsh veh • reesh mehr • keh • zee
the souvenir store	**Hediyelik eşya dükkanı**
	heh • dee • yeh • leek ehsh • yah
	dyuk • kah • nih
the supermarket	**Süpermarket**
	syu • pehr • mahr • keht
the tobacconist	**Tütüncü**
	tyu • tyun • jyu
the toy store	**Oyuncakçı**
	oh • yoon • jahk • chih

ASK AN ASSISTANT

When does the… open/close?	**…ne zaman açılıyor/kapanıyor?**
	…neh zah • mahn ah • chih • lih • yohr/
	kah • pah • nih • yohr
Where is…?	**…nerede?**
	…neh • reh • deh
the cashier [cash desk]	**Kasa**
	kah • sah
the escalator	**Yürüyen merdiven**
	yyu • ryu • yehn mehr • dee • vehn
the elevator [lift]	**Asansör**
	ah • sahn • surr
the fitting room	**Giyinme kabinleri**
	gee • yeen • meh kah • been • leh • ree
the store directory [guide]	**Mağaza rehberi**
	mah • ah • zah rehh • beh • ree
Can you help me?	**Bana yardım edebilir misiniz?**
	bah • nah yahr • dihm eh • deh • bee • leer
	mee • see • neez

I'm just looking.	**Sadece bakıyorum.**
	sah • deh • jeh bah • _kih_ • yoh • room
I'm being helped.	**Yardım alıyorum.**
	yahr • _dihm_ ah • _lih_ • yoh • room
Do you have any...?	**...var mı?**
	..._vahr_ mih
Can you show me...?	**...gösterebilir misiniz?** ...
	gurs • teh • reh • bee • _leer_
	mee • see • neez
Can you ship/	**Kargoyla yollayabilir/**
wrap it?	**Paketleyebilir misiniz?**
	kahr • _gohy_ • lah yohl • lah • yah • bee • _leer_/
	pah • _keht_ • leh • yeh • bee • _leer_
	mee • see • neez
How much?	**Ne kadar?**
	neh kah • dahr
That's all, thanks.	**Hepsi bu, teşekkürler.**
	hehp • see _boo_ teh • shehk • _kyur_ • lehr

For Souvenirs, see page 123.

PERSONAL PREFERENCES

I'd like something...	**...bir şey istiyorum.**
	...beer _shay_ ees • _tee_ • yoh • room
cheap/expensive	**Ucuz/Pahalı**
	oo • _jooz_/pah • _hah_ • lih
larger/smaller	**Daha büyük/küçük**
	dah • _hah_ byu • yyuk/kyu • chyuk
from this region	**Bu çevreden**
	boo chehv • reh • _dehn_
Is it real?	**Hakiki mi?**
	hah • kee • _kee_ mee
Could you show me	**Bunu/Onu bana gösterebilir misiniz?**
this/that?	boo • _noo_/oh • noo bah • nah
	gyus • teh • reh • bee • _leer_ mee • see • neez

That's not quite what I want.	**Bu tam istediğim gibi değil.** *boo <u>tahm</u> ees • teh • dee • <u>yeem</u> gee • bee deh • yeel*
I don't like it.	**Beğenmedim.** *beh • <u>yehn</u> • meh • deem*
That's too expensive.	**Çok pahalı.** *chohk pah • <u>hah</u> • lih*
I'd like to think about it.	**Biraz düşünmek istiyorum.** *<u>bee</u> • rahz dyu • shyun • <u>mehk</u> ees • <u>tee</u> • yoh • room*
I'll take it.	**Alıyorum.** *ah • <u>lih</u> • yoh • room*

> Major credit cards are commonly accepted, though not everywhere. It is a good idea to have some cash on hand, just in case. Note that some establishments also pass on the credit-processing costs, usually between 3-6%, as a surcharge.

PAYING & BARGAINING

How much?	**Ne kadar?** *<u>neh</u> kah • dahr*
I'll pay by…	**…ile ödeyeceğim.** *…ee • <u>leh</u> ur • deh • yeh • <u>jeh</u> • yeem*
in cash	**Nakit** *nah • <u>keet</u>*
by credit card	**Kredi kartı** *kreh • <u>dee</u> kahr • <u>tih</u>*
by traveler's check [cheque]	**Seyahat çeki** *seh • yah • <u>haht</u> cheh • <u>kee</u>*
A receipt, please.	**Fatura lütfen.** *fah • <u>too</u> • rah lyut • fehn*

That's too much.	**Çok pahalı.** _chohk_ pah • hah • _lih_
I'll give you...	**...veririm.** ...veh • _ree_ • reem
I only have...lira.	**Sadece...liram var.** _sah_ • deh • jeh..._lee_ • _rahm_ vahr
Is that your best price?	**En son fiyat bu mu?** ehn sohn fee • _yaht_ _boo_ moo
Give me a discount.	**Bana bir indirim yapın.** bah • _nah_ beer een • _deer_ • _reem_ yah • pihn

For Numbers, see page 20.

YOU MAY HEAR...

Nasıl ödeyeceksiniz? nah • _sihl_ ur • deh • yeh • _jehk_ • see • neez	How are you paying?
İşlem onaylanmadı/kabul edilmedi. eesh • _lehm_ oh • nie • _lahn_ • mah • dih/ kah • _bool_ eh • _deel_ • meh • dee	This transaction has not been approved/ accepted.
Başka bir kimlik kartınızı görebilir miyim? bahsh • _kah_ beer keem • _leek_ kahr • tih • nih • _zih_ gur • reh • bee • _leer_ mee • yeem	May I see another ID card?
Sadece nakit lütfen. _sah_ • deh • jeh nah • _keet_ _lyut_ • fehn	Cash only, please.
Bozuğunuz yok mu? boh • zoo • oo • _nooz_ _yohk_ moo	Do you have any smaller change?

MAKING A COMPLAINT

I'd like...	**...istiyorum.** ...ees • _tee_ • yoh • room

to exchange this	**Bunu değiştirmek**	
	boo • noo deh • yeesh • teer • mehk	
to return this	**Geri vermek**	
	geh • ree vehr • mehk	
a refund	**Paramı geri**	
	pah • rah • mih geh • ree	
to see the manager	**Müdürü görmek**	
	myu • dyu • ryu gurr • mehk	

SERVICES

Can you recommend…?	**…önerebilir misiniz?**	
	…ur • neh • reh • bee • leer mee • see • neez	
a barber	**Berber**	
	behr • behr	
a dry cleaner	**Kuru temizleyici**	
	koo • roo teh • meez leh • yee • jee	
a hairdresser	**Kuaför**	
	koo • ah • furr	
a laundromat [launderette]	**Çamaşırhane**	
	chah • mah • shihr • hah • neh	
a nail salon	**Güzellik salonu**	
	gyu • zehl • leek sah • loh • noo	

a spa	**Kaplıca**
	kahp • lih • _jah_
a travel agency	**Seyahat acentası**
	seh • yah • _haht_ ah • jehn • tah • _sih_
Can you...this?	**Bunu...misiniz?**
	boo • _noo_...mee • see • neez
alter	**değiştirebilir**
	deh • yeesh • tee • reh • bee • _leer_
clean	**temizleyebilir**
	teh • meez • leh • yeh • bee • _leer_
mend	**yamalayabilir**
	yah • mah • lah • yah • bee • _leer_
press	**ütüleyebilir**
	yu • tyu • leh • yeh • bee • _leer_
When will it be ready?	**Ne zaman hazır olacak?**
	neh zah • _mahn_ hah • _zihr_ oh • lah • _jahk_

HAIR & BEAUTY

I'd like...	**...istiyorum.**
	...ees • _tee_ • yoh • room
an appointment for today/ tomorrow	**Bugün/Yarın için bir randevu**
	boo • gyun/_yah_ • rihn ee • cheen beer _rahn_ • deh • _voo_
some color	**Boyama**
	boh • yah • _mah_
some highlights	**Röfle**
	rurf • _leh_
my hair styled	**Saç şekillendirme**
	sahch sheh • keel • lehn • deer • _meh_
a haircut	**Kestirmek**
	kehs • teer • _mehk_
a trim	**Uçlarından aldırmak**
	ooch • lah • rihn • _dahn_ ahl • dihr • _mahk_

(i)

Turkey is an excellent destination for visiting spas. There are many throughout the country and are recommended by the Turks as a means of natural therapy or a cure for certain ailments. There are many different treatments to enjoy: bathing in thermal springs, mud baths, wraps, massages and, the most famous of all, the Turkish bath. Turkish baths are a type of wet sauna or steam bath and have been known in Turkey for centuries. The concept was only exported to Europe around the mid-1800s.

If you are looking for a unique experience, consider visiting the hot springs in Kangal, located in the Sivas province, in Central Anatolia. In this thermal bath, mineral water flows in from five different springs and along with it so do innumerable small fish (small meaning about 1 to 5 inches long). Bathing with them is said to cure many skin illnesses.

Don't cut it too short.	**Çok kısa kesmeyin.**	
	chohk kih • sah kehs • meh • yeen	
Shorter here.	**Burayı kısaltın.**	
	boo • rah • yih kih • sahl • tihn	
an eyebrow/bikini wax	**Kaş aldırma/Ağda**	
	kahsh ahl • dih • mah/ah • dah	
a facial	**Yüz masajı**	
	yyuz mah • sah • jih	
a manicure/ pedicure	**Manikür/Pedikür**	
	mah • nee • kyur/peh • dee • kyur	
a (sports) massage	**Bir (spor) masajı**	
	beer (spohr) mah • sah • jih	
Do you do…?	**…yapar mısınız?**	
	…yah • pahr mih • sih • nihz	
acupuncture	**Akupunktur**	
	ah • koo • poonk • toor	

aromatherapy	**Aroma terapi**
	ah • roh • mah teh • rah • pee
oxygen treatment	**Oksijen tedavisi**
	ohk • see • jehn teh • dah • vee • see
Is there a sauna?	**Sauna var mı?**
	sah • oo • nah vahr mih

ANTIQUES

How old is this?	**Bu ne kadar eski?**
	boo neh kah • dahr ehs • kee
Will I have problems with customs?	**Gümrükte sorun çıkar mı?**
	gyum • ryuk • teh soh • roon chih • kahr mih
Is there a certificate of authenticity?	**Hakikilik belgesi var mı?**
	hah • kee • kee • leek behl • geh • see vahr mih

CLOTHING

I'd like…	**…istiyorum.**
	…ees • tee • yoh • room
Can I try this on?	**Bunu deneyebilir miyim?**
	boo • noo deh • neh • yeh • bee • leer mee • yeem
It doesn't fit.	**Olmadı.**
	ohl • mah • dih
It's too…	**Çok…**
	chohk…
big	**büyük**
	byu • yyuk
small	**küçük**
	kyu • chyuk
short	**kısa**
	kih • sah

long	**uzun**
	oo • zoon
Do you have this in size…?	**Bunun…bedeni var mı?**
	boo • noon…beh • deh • nee vahr mih
Do you have this in a bigger/smaller size?	**Bunun daha büyük/küçük bedeni var mı?**
	boo • noon dah • hah byu • yyuk/ kyu • chyuk beh • deh • nee vahr mih

For Numbers, see page 20.

YOU MAY SEE…

ERKEK GİYİMİ	men's clothing
BAYAN GİYİMİ	women's clothing
ÇOCUK GİYİMİ	children's clothing

COLORS

| I'm looking for something in… | **…bir şeyler arıyorum.** |
| | *…beer shay • lehr ah • rih • yoh • room* |

beige	**Bej**
	behj
black	**Siyah**
	see • yah
blue	**Mavi**
	mah • vee
brown	**Kahverengi**
	kah • veh • rehn • gee
green	**Yeşil**
	yeh • sheel
gray	**Gri**
	gree
orange	**Portakal rengi**
	pohr • tah • kahl rehn • gee
pink	**Pembe**
	pehm • beh
purple	**Mor**
	mohr
red	**Kırmızı**
	kihr • mih • zih
white	**Beyaz**
	beh • yahz
yellow	**Sarı**
	sah • rih

CLOTHES & ACCESSORIES

backpack	**sırt çantası**
	sihrt chahn • tah • sih
belt	**kemer**
	keh • mehr
bikini	**bikini**
	bee • kee • nee
blouse	**bluz**
	blooz

bra	**sütyen**
	syut • yehn
briefs [underpants]	**külot**
	kyu • loht
coat	**palto**
	pahl • toh
dress	**elbise**
	ehl • bee • seh
hat	**şapka**
	shahp • kah
jacket	**ceket**
	jeh • keht
jeans	**kot pantalon**
	koht pahn • tah • lohn
pajamas	**pijama**
	pee • jah • mah
pants [trousers]	**pantalon**
	pahn • tah • lohn
pantyhose [tights]	**tayt**
	tiet
purse [handbag]	**el çantası**
	ehl chahn • tah • sih
raincoat	**yağmurluk**
	yah • moor • look

scarf	**eşarp**
	eh • shahrp
shirt (men's)	**gömlek**
	gurm • lehk
shorts	**şort**
	shohrt
skirt	**etek**
	eh • tehk
socks	**çorap**
	choh • rahp
suit	**takım elbise**
	tah • kihm ehl • bee • seh
sunglasses	**güneş gözlüğü**
	gyu • nehsh gurz • lyu • yyu
sweater	**süveter**
	syu • veh • tehr
sweatshirt	**sweatshirt**
	sveht • shurrt
swimming trunks/ swimsuit	**mayo**
	mah • yoh
T-shirt	**tişört**
	tee • shurrt
tie	**kravat**
	krah • vaht

| underwear | **külot** |
| | *kyu • loht* |

FABRIC

I'd like...	**...istiyorum.**
	...ees • tee • yoh • room
cotton	**Pamuklu**
	pah • mook • loo
denim	**Kot kumaşı**
	koht koo • mah • shih
lace	**Dantel**
	dahn • tehl
leather	**Deri**
	deh • ree
linen	**Keten**
	keh • tehn
silk	**İpek**
	ee • pehk
wool	**Yün**
	yyun
Is it machine washable?	**Makinede yıkanabilir mi?**
	mah • kee • neh • deh yih • kah • nah • bee • leer mee

SHOES

I'd like…	**…istiyorum.** …ees • *tee* • yoh • room
high-heeled/ flat shoes	**Yüksek topuklu/Düz taban ayakkabı** *yuk* • sehk toh • pook • *loo*/ dyuz tah • *bahn* ah • *yahk* • kah • bih
boots	**Çizme** *cheez* • meh
loafers	**Mokasen** moh • kah • *sehn*
sandals	**Sandalet** sahn • dah • *leht*
shoes	**Ayakkabı** ah • *yahk* • kah • bih
slippers	**Terlik** *tehr* • leek
sneakers	**Koşu ayakkabısı** koh • *shoo* ah • *yahk* • kah • bih • sih
In size…	**…numara.** …noo • *mah* • rah

For Numbers, see page 20.

SIZES

small	**küçük** kyu • *chyuk*
medium	**orta** ohr • *tah*
large	**büyük** byu • *yyuk*
extra large	**çok büyük** chohk byu • *yyuk*

petite	**ufak**
	oo • fahk
plus size	**battal boy**
	baht • tahl boy

NEWSAGENT & TOBACCONIST

Do you sell English-language books/newspapers?	**İngilizce kitap/gazete satıyor musunuz?**
	een • gee • leez • jeh kee • tahp/
	gah • zeh • teh sah • tih • yohr
	moo • soo • nooz
I'd like...	**...istiyorum.**
	...ees • tee • yoh • room
candy [sweets]	**Şeker**
	sheh • kehr
chewing gum	**Sakız**
	sah • kihz
a chocolate bar	**Çikolata**
	chee • koh • lah • tah
cigars	**Puro**
	poo • roh
a pack/carton of cigarettes	**Paket/Karton sigara**
	pah • keht/cahr • tohn see • gah • rah

a lighter	**Çakmak**
	chahk • mahk
a magazine	**Dergi**
	dehr • gee
matches	**Kibrit**
	keeb • reet
a newspaper	**Gazete**
	gah • zeh • teh
a road/town map of...	**...yol/kent haritası**
	...yohl/kehnt hah • ree • tah • sih
stamps	**Pul**
	pool

(i)

You can find many English-language newspapers at newsstands in major cities, at airports and bus and train stations.

PHOTOGRAPHY

| I'm looking for... camera. | **...bir fotoğraf makinesi arıyorum.** |
| | *...beer foh • toh • rahf mah • kee • neh • se ah • rih • yoh • room* |

an automatic	**Otomatik**
	oh • toh • mah • <u>teek</u>
a digital	**Dijital**
	dee • jee • <u>tahl</u>
a disposable	**Tek kullanımlık**
	<u>tehk</u> kool • <u>lah</u> • nihm • lihk
I'd like...	**...istiyorum.**
	...ees • <u>tee</u> • yoh • room
a battery	**Pil**
	peel
digital prints	**Dijital baskı**
	dee • jee • <u>tahl</u> bahs • <u>kih</u>
a memory card	**Hafıza kartı**
	hah • fih • <u>zah</u> kahr • <u>tih</u>
Can I print digital photos here?	**Dijital fotoğrafları burda basabilir miyim?**
	dee • jee • <u>tahl</u> foh • toh • <u>rahf</u> • lah • rih boor • dah bah • sah • bee • <u>leer</u> mee • yeem

SOUVENIRS

bottle of wine	**bir şişe şarap**
	beer shee • <u>sheh</u> shah • <u>rahp</u>
box of chocolates	**kutu çikolata**
	koo • <u>too</u> chee • koh • <u>lah</u> • tah

calendar	**takvim**
	tahk • veem
carpets	**halı**
	hah • lih
dolls	**bebek**
	beh • behk
jewelry	**mücevher**
	myu • jehv • hehr
key ring	**anahtarlık**
	ah • nahh • tahr • lihk
lace	**dantel**
	dahn • tehl
leather goods	**deri eşyalar**
	deh • ree ehsh • yah • lahr
perfume	**parfüm**
	pahr • fyum
porcelain	**porselen**
	pohr • seh • lehn
postcards	**kartpostal**
	kahrt • pohs • tahl
pottery	**çömlek**
	churm • lehk
rug	**kilim**
	kee • leem

scarf	**eşarp**
	eh • shahrp
silk garments	**ipek eşya**
	ee • pehk ehsh • yah
souvenir guide	**hediyelik eşya rehberi**
	heh • dee • yeh • leek ehsh • yah
	reh • beh • ree
T-shirt	**tişört**
	tee • shurrt
tea towel	**kurulama bezi**
	koo • roo • lah • mah beh • zee
Can I see this/that?	**Buna/Şuna bakabilir miyim?**
	boo • nah/shoo • nah bah • kah • bee • leer
	mee • yeem
It's the one in the window/display case.	**Vitrindeki./Sergilenen.**
	veet • reen • deh • kee/sehr • gee • leh • nehn
I'd like…	**…istiyorum.**
	…ees • tee • yoh • room
a battery	**Pil**
	peel
a bracelet	**Bilezik**
	bee • leh • zeek
a brooch	**Broş**
	brohsh

For everything under one roof, be sure to go shopping in the **Kapalı Çarsi** (covered market or Grand Bazaar) in Istanbul. One of the largest covered markets in the world, there are literally thousands of shops and restaurants selling just about anything imaginable. Here you'll be able to find lots of Turkish souvenirs to take back home with you and it's a great chance to practice your haggling skills! Be sure to enjoy the ambiance, but stay alert for pickpockets and bag snatchers.

earrings	**Küpe**
	kyu • peh
a necklace	**Kolye**
	kohl • yeh
a ring	**Yüzük**
	yyu • zyuk
a watch	**Kol saati**
	kohl sah • ah • tee
copper	**Bakır**
	bah • kihr
crystal	**Kuartz**
	koo • ahrtz
diamond	**Elmas**
	ehl • mahs
white/yellow gold	**Beyaz/Sarı altın**
	beh • yahz/sah • rih ahl • tihn
pearl	**İnci**
	een • jee
pewter	**Kurşun-kalay alaşımı**
	koor • shoon kah • lie ah • lah • shih • mih
platinum	**Platin**
	plah • teen
sterling silver	**Som gümüş**
	sohm gyu • myush
Is this real?	**Hakiki mi?**
	hah • kee • kee mee
Can you engrave it?	**İşleyebilir misin?**
	eesh • leh • yeh • bee • leer mee • seen

SPORT & LEISURE

NEED TO KNOW

When's the game?	**Maç kaçta?**
	mahch kahch • tah
Where's...?	**...nerede?**
	...neh • reh • deh
the beach	**Plaj**
	plahj
the park	**Park**
	pahrk
the pool	**Yüzme havuzu**
	yyuz • meh hah • voo • zoo
Is it safe to swim/ dive here?	**Burada yüzmek/dalmak güvenli mi?**
	boo • rah • dah yyuz • mehk/dahl • mahk gyu • vehn • lee mee
Can I rent [hire] golf clubs?	**Golf sopalarını kiralayabilir miyim?**
	gohlf soh • pah • lah • rih • nih kee • rah • lah • yah • bee • leer mee • yeem
How much per hour?	**Saatlik ücreti nedir?**
	sah • aht • leek yuj • reh • tee neh • deer
How far is it to...?	**...buradan ne kadar uzakta?**
	boo • rah • dahn neh kah • dahr oo • zahk • tah
Can you show me on the map?	**Bana haritada gösterebilir misiniz?**
	bah • nah hah • ree • tah • dah gurs • teh • reh • bee • leer mee • see • neez

WATCHING SPORT

When's...?	**...ne zaman?**
	...neh zah • mahn
the basketball game	**Basketbol maçı**
	bahs • keht • bohl mah • chih
the boxing match	**Boks maçı**
	bohks mah • chih
the cycling race	**Bisiklet yarışı**
	bee • seek • leht yah • rih • shih
the golf tournament	**Golf turnuvası**
	gohlf toor • noo • vah • sih
the soccer game	**Futbol maçı**
	foot • bohl mah • chih
the tennis match	**Tenis maçı**
	teh • nees mah • chih
the volleyball game	**Voleybol maçı**
	voh • lay • bohl mah • chih
Which teams are playing?	**Hangi takımlar oynuyor?**
	hahn • gee tah • kihm • lahr oy • noo • yohr
Where's...?	**...nerede?**
	...neh • reh • deh
the horsetrack	**At yarışı**
	aht yah • rih • shih
the racetrack	**Hipodrom**
	hee • pohd • rohm
the stadium	**Stadyum**
	stah • dyoom
Where can I place a bet?	**Nerede bahis oynayabilirim?**
	neh • reh • deh bah • hees oy • nah • yah • bee • lee • reem

PLAYING SPORT

Since Turkey is surrounded by so much water, it is no surprise that water sports are popular. Swimming, sailing, scuba diving and windsurfing are common in the seas, while one can go rafting or canoeing on one of Turkey's many rivers. Other sports like caving and trekking can be enjoyed in addition to golf or horseback riding. The national sports, however, are soccer and wrestling. Oil wrestling has in fact been practiced since Ottoman times.

Where's…?	**…nerede?**
	…_neh_ • reh • deh
the golf course	**Golf sahası**
	gohlf sah • hah • sih
the gym	**Spor klübü**
	spohr klyu • byu
the park	**Park**
	pahrk
the tennis courts	**Tenis kortları**
	teh • _nees_ kohrt • lah • rih

How much per...?	...ücreti nedir?
	...yuj • reh • <u>tee neh</u> • deer
day	**Günlük**
	gyun • <u>lyuk</u>
hour	**Saatlik**
	sah • aht • <u>leek</u>
game	**Bir oyun**
	beer oh • <u>yoon</u>
round	**Bir tur**
	beer toor
Can I rent [hire]...?	...kiralayabilir miyim?
	...kee • rah • lah • yah • bee • <u>leer</u>
	mee • yeem
golf clubs	**Sopa**
	soh • <u>pah</u>
equipment	**Donanım**
	doh • nah • <u>nihm</u>
a racket	**Raket**
	rah • <u>keht</u>

AT THE BEACH/POOL

Where's the beach/ pool?	**Plaj/Havuz nerede?**
	plahj/hah • <u>vooz</u> <u>neh</u> • reh • deh

Is there...?	**Burada...var mı?**
	boo • rah • dah...vahr mih
a kiddie [paddling] pool	**çocuk havuzu**
	choh • _jook_ hah • voo • zoo
an indoor/outdoor pool	**kapalı/açık havuz**
	kah • pah • _lih_/ah • _chihk_ hah • _vooz_
a lifeguard	**cankurtaran**
	jan • _koor_ • tah • rahn
Is it safe...?	**...güvenli mi?**
	...gyu • vehn • _lee_ mee
to swim	**Yüzmek**
	yyuz • _mehk_
to dive	**Dalmak**
	dahl • _mahk_
for children	**Çocuklar için**
	choh • _jook_ • lahr ee • cheen
want to rent [hire]...	**...Kiralamak istiyorum.** ...
	kee • rah • lah • _mahk_ ees • _tee_ • yoh • room
a deck chair	**Katlanabilir koltuk**
	kaht • lah • nah • bee • _leer_ kohl • _took_
diving equipment	**Dalış donanımı**
	dah • _lihsh_ doh • _nah_ • nih • mih
a jet-ski	**Jet ski**
	jeht skee
a motorboat	**Deniz motoru**
	deh • _neez_ moh • toh • _roo_
a rowboat	**Sandal**
	sahn • _dahl_
snorkeling equipment	**Şnorkel takımı**
	shnohr • kehl tah • _kih_ • mih
a surfboard	**Surf tahtası**
	surrf _tah_ • htah • _sih_
a towel	**Havlu**
	hahv • _loo_

an umbrella	**Şemsiye**
	shehm • see • ih
water skis	**Su kayağı**
	soo kah • _yah_ • ih
windsurfer	**Rüzgar sörfçüsü**
	ryuz • _gahr_ surrf • chyu • syu

WINTER SPORTS

YOU MAY SEE...

ÇEKİCİ TELEFERİK	drag lift
TELEFERİK	cable car
KOLTUKLU TELEFERİK	chair lift
ACEMİ	novice
ORTA SEVİYEDE	intermediate
UZMAN	expert
PİST KAPALI	trail [piste] closed

A lift pass for a day/	**Bir/Beş günlük teleferik pasosu lütfen.**
five days, please.	beer/behsh gyun • lyuk teh • leh • feh • reek
	pah • soh • soo lyut • fehn

Though most people associate Turkey with a hot climate, Turkey is actually quite mountainous and there is very good skiing to be enjoyed throughout the country. The following is a list of the major ski resorts and their locations: Ankara – Elmadag, outside of Ankara; Antalya – Saklikent, northwest of Antalya; Bolu-Kartalkaya, off the Istanbul – Ankara highway; Bursa – Uludag, just south of Bursa; Erzurum-Palandoken, near Erzurum; Ilgaz Dagi, between Kastamonu and Cankiri; Kars – Sarikamis, close to Kars; Kayseri – Erciyes, near Kayseri and Zigana – Gumushane, just outside of Gumushane.

I want to rent [hire]…	**…kiralamak istiyorum.**	…kee • rah • lah • mahk ees • _tee_ • yoh • room
boots	**Kayak çizmesi**	kah • _yahk_ _cheez_ • meh • see
a helmet	**Kask**	kahsk
poles	**Kayak sopası**	kah • _yahk_ soh • pah • sih
skis	**Kayak**	kah • _yahk_
a snowboard	**Kar kayağı**	_kahr_ kah • yah • ih
snowshoes	**Kar ayakkabısı**	_kahr_ ah • yahk • kah • bih • sih
These are too big/ small.	**Bunlar çok büyük/küçük.**	boon • _lahr_ _chohk_ byu • _yyuk_/kyu • _chyuk_
Are there lessons?	**Ders var mı?**	dehrs _vahr_ mih

I'm a beginner.	**Yeni başlıyorum.** *yeh • nee bahsh • lih • yoh • room*
I'm experienced.	**Deneyimliyim.** *deh • neh • yeem • lee • yeem*
A trail [piste] map, please.	**Pist haritası lütfen.** *peest hah • ree • tah • sih lyut • fehn*

OUT IN THE COUNTRY

I'd like a map of…	**…haritası istiyorum.** *…hah • ree • tah • sih ees • tee • yoh • room*
this region	**Bu bölge** *boo burl • geh*
walking routes	**Yürüyüş yolları** *yyu • ryu • yyush yohl • lah • rih*
bike routes	**Bisiklet yolları** *bee • see • kleht yohl • lah • rih*
the trails	**Dar yollar** *dahr yohl • lahr*
Is it easy?	**Kolay mı?** *koh • lie mih*
Is it difficult?	**Zor mu?** *zohr moo*
Is it far?	**Uzak mı?** *oo • zahk mih*
Is it steep?	**Dik mi?** *deek mee*
How far is it to…?	**…ne kadar uzakta?** *…neh kah • dahr oo • zahk • tah*
Can you show me on the map?	**Bana haritada gösterebilir misiniz?** *bah • nah hah • ree • tah • dah gurs • teh • reh • bee • leer mee • see • neez*
I'm lost.	**Kayboldum.** *kie • bohl • doom*

Where's…?	…nerede?
	…<u>neh</u> • reh • deh
the bridge	**Köprü**
	kurp • <u>ryu</u>
the cave	**Mağara**
	mah • <u>ah</u> • rah
the cliff	**Uçurum**
	oo • choo • <u>room</u>
the desert	**Çöl**
	<u>churl</u>
the farm	**Çiftlik**
	cheeft • <u>leek</u>
the field	**Tarla**
	tahr • <u>lah</u>
the forest	**Orman**
	ohr • <u>mahn</u>
the hill	**Tepe**
	teh • <u>peh</u>
the lake	**Göl**
	gurl
the mountain	**Dağ**
	dah
the nature preserve	**Milli park**
	meel • <u>lee</u> pahrk

the overlook	**Hakim tepe**
	hah • keem teh • peh
the park	**Park**
	pahrk
the path	**Patika**
	pah • tee • kah
the peak	**Tepe**
	teh • peh
the picnic area	**Piknik alanı**
	peek • neek ah • lah • nih
the pond	**Gölcük**
	gurl • jyuk
the river	**Irmak**
	ihr • mahk
the sea	**Deniz**
	deh • neez
the thermal springs	**Termal kaynaklar**
	tehr • mahl kie • nahk • lahr
the stream	**Dere**
	deh • reh
the valley	**Vadi**
	vah • dee
the vineyard/ winery	**Bağ/Şaraphane**
	bah/shah • rahp • hah • neh
the waterfall	**Şelale**
	sheh • lah • leh

TRAVELING WITH CHILDREN

NEED TO KNOW

Is there a discount for children?	**Çocuklar için indirim var mı?** *choh • jook • lahr ee • cheen een • dee • reem vahr mih*
Can you recommend a babysitter?	**Bir çocuk bakıcısı önerebilir misiniz?** *beer choh • jook bah • kih • jih • sih ur • neh • reh • bee • leer mee • see • neez*
Could we have a a child's seat/ highchair?	**Çocuk sandalyesi/Yüksek sandalye alabilir miyiz?** *choh • jook sahn • dahl • yeh • see/ yyuk • sehk sahn • dahl • yeh ah • lah • bee • leer mee • yeez*
Where can I change the baby?	**Bebeğin altını nerede değiştirebilirim?** *beh • beh • yeen ahl • tih • nih neh • reh • deh deh • yeesh • tee • reh • bee • lee • reem*

OUT & ABOUT

Can you recommend something for the kids?	**Çocuklar için birşeyler önerir misiniz?** *choh • jook • lahr ee • cheen beer • shay • lehr ur • neh • reer mee • see • neez*
Where's...?	**...nerede?** ... *neh • reh • deh*
the amusement park	**Oyun parkı** *oh • yoon pahr • kih*
the arcade	**Oyun salonu** *oh • yoon sah • loh • noo*

the kiddie	**Çocuk havuzu**
[paddling] pool	choh • _jook_ hah • voo • _zoo_
the park	**Park**
	pahrk
the playground	**Çocuk parkı**
	choh • _jook_ pahr • _kih_
the zoo	**Hayvanat bahçesi**
	hie • vah • _naht_ bah • cheh • _see_
Are kids allowed?	**Çocuklara serbest mi?**
	choh • _jook_ • lah • _rah_ sehr • _behst_ mee
Is it safe for kids?	**Çocuklar için güvenli mi?**
	choh • _jook_ • lahr ee • cheen
	gyu • _vehn_ • lee mee
Is it suitable for…	**…yaş için uygun mu?**
year olds?	…_yash_ ee • cheen ooy • _goon_ moo

For Numbers, see page 20.

BABY ESSENTIALS

Do you have…?	**…var mı?**
	…_vahr_ mih
a baby bottle	**Biberon**
	bee • beh • _rohn_

baby wipes	**Bebek mendili**
	beh • _behk_ mehn • dee • _lee_
a car seat	**Araba koltuğu**
	ah • rah • _bah_ kohl • too • oo
a children's menu/ portion	**Çocuk menüsü/porsiyonu**
	choh • _jook_ meh • nyu • _syu_/ pohr • see • yoh • _noo_
a child's seat	**Çocuk sandalyesi**
	choh • _jook_ sahn • dahl • yeh • _see_
a cot	**Çocuk Beşik**
	choh • _jook_ beh • sheek
a crib	**Çocuk yatağı**
	choh • _jook_ yah • _tah_ • ih

diapers [nappies]	**Bebek bezi**
	beh • <u>bek</u> beh • zee
formula	**Formül**
	fohr • <u>myul</u>
a highchair	**Çocuk Yüksek sandalye**
	choh • <u>jook</u> yyuk • <u>sehk</u> sahn • dahl • <u>yeh</u>
a pacifier [dummy]	**Yatıştırıcı**
	yah • tihsh • tih • rih • <u>jih</u>
a playpen	**Portatif çocuk parkı**
	pohr • tah • <u>teef</u> choh • <u>jook</u> pahr • kih
a stroller	**Puset**
[push chair]	*poo • <u>seht</u>*
Can I breastfeed the baby here?	**Bebeği burda emzirebilir miyim?**
	beh • beh • <u>yee</u> boor • dah ehm • zee • reh • bee • <u>leer</u> mee • yeem
Where can I change the baby?	**Bebeğin altını nerede değiştirebilirim?**
	beh • beh • <u>yeen</u> ahl • tih • <u>nih</u> <u>neh</u> • reh • deh deh • yeesh • tee • reh • bee • lee • reem

For Dining with Children, see page 175.

BABYSITTING

Can you recommend a babysitter?	**Bir çocuk bakıcısı önerebilir misiniz?**
	beer choh • jook bah • kih • jih • sih ur • neh • reh • bee • leer mee • see • neez
What's the charge?	**Ücreti nedir?**
	yuj • reh • tee neh • deer
We'll be back by…	**…kadar geri döneriz.**
	…kah • dahr geh • ree dur • neh • reez
I can be reached at…	**Bana…ulaşabilirsiniz.**
	bah • nah… oo • lah • shah • bee • leer • see • neez

HEALTH & SAFETY

EMERGENCIES	144
POLICE	146
HEALTH	148
PHARMACY	156
DISABLED TRAVELERS	161

EMERGENCIES

NEED TO KNOW

Help!	**İmdat!**
	eem • daht
Go away!	**Çekil git!**
	cheh • keel geet
Stop thief!	**Durdurun, hırsız!**
	door • doo • roon hihr • sihz
Get a doctor!	**Bir doktor bulun!**
	beer dohk • tohr boo • loon
Fire!	**Yangın!**
	yahn • gihn
I'm lost.	**Kayboldum.**
	kie • bohl • doom
Can you help me?	**Bana yardım edebilir misiniz?**
	bah • nah yahr • dihm
	eh • deh • bee • leer mee • see • neez

YOU MAY HEAR...

Bu formu doldurun lütfen.
boo <u>fohr</u> • moo dohl • doo • roon
<u>lyut</u> • fehn

Please fill
out this
form.

Kimliğiniz lütfen.
keem • lee • yee • <u>neez</u> <u>lyut</u> • fehn

Your identification,
please.

Ne zaman/Nerede oldu?
<u>neh</u> zah • mahn/<u>neh</u> • reh • deh
ohl • doo

When/Where did it
happen?

Nasıl biriydi?
<u>nah</u> • sihl bee • <u>reey</u> • dee

What did he/she
look like?

POLICE

NEED TO KNOW

Call the police!	**Polis çağırın!**
	poh • _lees_ chah • _ih_ • rihn
Where's the police station?	**Karakol nerede?**
	kah • rah • _kohl_ _neh_ • reh • deh
There has been an accident/attack.	**Bir kaza/saldırı oldu.**
	beer kah • _zah_/sahl • _dih_ • rih ohl • doo
My child is missing.	**Çocuğum kayıp.**
	choh • joo • _oom_ kah • _yihp_
I need…	**…ihtiyacım var.** …
	eeh • tee • yah • _jihm_ vahr
an interpreter	**Tercümana**
	tehr • jyu • mah • _nah_
to contact my lawyer	**Avukatımla görüşmeye**
	ah • voo • kah • _tihm_ • lah _gur_ • ryush • meh • _yeh_
to make a phone call	**Telefon görüşmesi yapmaya**
	teh • leh • _fohn_ gur • ryush • meh • _see_ yahp • mah • _yah_
I'm innocent.	**Masumum.**
	mah • _soo_ • moom

CRIME & LOST PROPERTY

I want to report…	**Bir…haber vermek istiyorum.**
	beer…hah • _behr_ vehr • mehk ees • _tee_ • yoh • room

a mugging	**gasp**
	gahsp
a rape	**tecavüz**
	teh • jah • vyuz
a theft	**hırsızlık**
	hihr • sihz • lihk
I've been robbed/ mugged.	**Çarpıldım/Soyuldum.**
	chah • rpihl • dihm/soh • yool • doom
I've lost my…	**…kaybettim.**
	…kie • beht • teem
My…has been stolen.	**…çalındı.**
	…chah • lihn • dih
backpack	**Sırt çantam**
	sihrt chahn • tahm
bicycle	**Bisikletim**
	bee • seek • leh • teem
camera	**Fotoğraf makinem**
	foh • toh • rahf mah • kee • nehm
(rental) car	**(Kiralık) Arabam**
	(kee • rah • lihk) ah • rah • bahm
computer	**Bilgisayarım**
	beel • gee • sah • yah • rihm
credit card	**Kredi kartlarım**
	kreh • dee kahrt • lah • rihm
jewelry	**Mücevheratım**
	myu • jehv • heh • rah • tihm
money	**Param**
	pah • rahm
passport	**Pasaportum**
	pah • sah • pohr • toom
purse [handbag]	**Cüzdanım**
	jyuz • dah • nihm
traveler's checks [cheques]	**Seyahat çeklerim**
	seh • yah • haht chehk • leh • reem

wallet	**Cüzdanım** *jyuz • dah • nihm*
I need a police report.	**Polis raporuna ihtiyacım var.** *poh • lees rah • poh • rooh • nah* *eeh • tee • yah • jihm vahr*
Where is the British/ American/Irish embassy?	**İngiliz/Amerikan/İrlanda büyükelçiliği** **nerede?** *een • geeh • leez/ah • meh • rih • kahn/* *ehr • lahn • dah* *byu • yuhk • ehl • chee • lih • ee* *neh • reh • deh*

HEALTH

NEED TO KNOW

I'm sick [ill].	**Hastayım.** *hahs • tah • yihm*
I need an English- speaking doctor.	**İngilizce konuşan bir doktora ihtiyacım var.** *een • gee • leez • jeh koh • noo • shahn* *beer dohk • toh • rah* *eeh • tee • yah • jihm vahr*
It hurts here.	**Burası acıyor.** *boo • rah • sih ah • jih • yohr*
I have a stomachache.	**Mide ağrım var.** *mee • deh ah • rihm vahr*

FINDING A DOCTOR

Can you recommend a doctor/dentist?	**Bir doktor/dişçi önerir misiniz?** *beer dohk • tohr/deesh • chee* *ur • neh • reer mee • see • neez*

Could the doctor to see me here?	**Doktor beni gelip burada görebilir mi?**
	dohk • _tohr_ beh • _nee_ geh • _leep_
	boo • rah • dah gur • reh • bee • _leer_ mee
I need an English-speaking doctor.	**İngilizce konuşan bir doktora ihtiyacım var.**
	een • gee • _leez_ • jeh koh • noo • _shahn_ beer
	dohk • toh • _rah_ eeh • tee • yah • _jihm_ vahr
What are the office hours?	**Çalışma saatleri nedir?**
	chah • lihsh • _mah_ sah • aht • leh • _ree_
	neh • deer
Can I make an appointment…?	**…için randevu alabilir miyim?**
	…ee • _cheen_ rahn • deh • _voo_
	ah • lah • bee • _leer_ mee • yeem
for today	**Bugün**
	boo • gyun
for tomorrow	**Yarın**
	yah • _rihn_
as soon as possible	**En yakın zaman**
	ehn yah • _kihn_ zah • _mahn_
It's urgent.	**Acil.**
	ah • _jeel_

SYMPTOMS

I'm bleeding.	**Kanamam var.**
	kah • nah • _mahm_ vahr
I'm constipated.	**Kabızım.**
	kah • _bih_ • zihm
I'm dizzy.	**Başım dönüyor.**
	bah • _shihm_ dur • _nyu_ • yohr
I'm nauseous/vomiting.	**Bulantım var./Kusuyorum.**
	boo • lahn • _tihm_ vahr/
	koo • _soo_ • yoh • room
It hurts here.	**Burası acıyor.**
	boo • rah • _sih_ ah • _jih_ • yohr
I have…	**…var.**
	…vahr

an allergic reaction	**Alerjik reaksiyonum**
	ah • lehr • jeek reh • ahk • see • yoh • noon
chest pain	**Göğüs ağrım**
	gur • yus ah • rihm
an earache	**Kulak ağrım**
	koo • lahk ah • rihm
a fever	**Ateşim**
	ah • teh • sheem
pain	**Ağrım**
	ah • rihm
a rash	**Kaşıntım**
	kah • shihn • tihm
a sprain	**Burkulmam**
	boor • kool • mahm
some swelling	**Şişliğim**
	sheesh • lee • eem
a stomachache	**Mide ağrım**
	mee • deh ah • rihm
sunstroke	**Güneş çarpmam**
	gyu • nehsh chahrp • mahm
I've been sick [ill] for…days.	**…gündür hastayım.**
	…gyun • dyur hahs • tah • yihm

For Numbers, see page 20.

CONDITIONS

I'm...	**Ben...**
	ben
anemic	**anemi hastasıyım**
	ah • neh • mee hahs • tah • sih • yihm
asthmatic	**astım**
	ahs • tihm
diabetic	**şeker hastasıyım**
	sheh • kehr hahs • tah • sih • yihm
epileptic	**sara hastasıyım**
	sah • rah has • tah • sih • yihm
I'm allergic to antibiotics/penicillin.	**Antibiyotiğe/Penisiline alerjim var.**
	ahn • tee • bee • yoh • tee • yeh/
	peh • nee • see • lee • neh ah • lehr • jeem vahr
I have arthritis.	**Artiritim.**
	ahr • tee • ree • teem
I have (high/low) blood pressure.	**(Yüksek/Düşük) Tansiyonum var.**
	(yyuk • sehk/dyu • shyuk)
	tahn • see • yoh • noom vahr
I have a heart condition.	**Kalbimden rahatsızım.**
	kahl • beem • dehn rah • hat • sih • zihm
I'm on...	**...dayım.**
	...dah • yihm

TREATMENT

Do I need prescription/medicine?	**Reçeteye/ilaca ihtiyacım var mı?**
	reh • cheh • teh • yeh/ee • lah • jah
	eeh • tee • yah • jihm vahr mih
Can you prescribe a generic drug? [unbranded medication]?	**Genel bir ilaç yazabilir misiniz?**
	geh • nehl beer ee • lahch
	yah • zah • bee • leer mee • see • neez

YOU MAY HEAR...

Sorununuz ne?	What's
soh•roo•noo•nooz neh	wrong?
Neresi acıyor?	Where does it
neh•reh•see ah•jih•yohr	hurt?
Burası acıyor mu?	Does it hurt
boo•rah•sih ah•jih•yohr moo	here?
Başka ilaç alıyor musunuz?	Are you taking
bahsh•kah ee•lahch ah•lih•yohr	any other
moo•soo•nooz	medication?
Herhangi bir şeye alerjiniz var mı?	Are you allergic
hehr•hahn•gee beer sheh•yeh	to anything?
ah•lehr•jee•neez vahr mih	
Ağzınızı açın.	Open your
ah•zih•nih•zih ah•chihn	mouth.
Derin nefes alın.	Breathe deeply.
deh•reen neh•fes ah•lihn	
Hastaneye gitmenizi istiyorum.	I want you to go
hahs•tah•neh•yeh geet•meh•nee•zee	to the hospital.
ees•tee•yoh•room	

Where can I get it?	**Nereden alabilirim?**
	neh•reh•den ah•lah•bee•lee•reem

For Pharmacy, see page 156.

HOSPITAL

Please notify my family.	**Lütfen aileme bildirin.**
	lyut•fehn ah•ee•leh•meh
	beel•dee•reen

in pain.	**Acı içindeyim.**
	ah • jih ee • cheen • deh • yeem
eed a doctor/	**Doktora/Hemşireye ihtiyacım var.**
urse.	*dohk • toh • rah/hehm • shee • reh • yeh*
	eeh • tee • yah • jihm vahr
hen are visiting	**Ziyaret saatleri ne zaman?**
urs?	*zee • yah • reht sah • aht • leh • ree neh*
	zah • mahn
n visiting…	**…ziyaret edeceğim.**
	…zee • yah • reht eh • deh • jeh • yeem

DENTIST

e broken a tooth/	**Dişim kırıldı./Dolgumu düşürdüm.**
st a filling.	*dee • sheem kih • rihl • dih/dohl • goo • moo*
	dyu • shyur • dyum
ave a toothache.	**Dişim ağrıyor.**
	dee • sheem ah • rih • yohr
an you fix this	**Bu protezi onarabilir misiniz?**
enture?	*boo proh • teh • zee*
	oh • nah • rah • bee • leer
	mee • see • neez

GYNECOLOGIST

I have menstrual cramps.	**Aybaşı ağrım.** _ie_ • bah • shih ah • rihm
I have a vaginal infection.	**Vajina iltihaplanması var.** vah • jee • _nah_ eel • tee • hahp • lahn • mah • _sih_ vahr
I missed my period.	**Günüm gecikti.** gyu • _nyum_ geh • jeek • _tee_
I'm on the Pill.	**Doğum kontrol hapı kullanıyorum.** doh • _oom_ kohnt • rohl hah • _pih_ kool • lah • _nih_ • yoh • room
I'm not pregnant.	**Hamile değilim.** hah • mee • _leh_ deh • _yee_ • leem
I'm ... months pregnant.	**...aylık hamileyim** ...ahy • lihk hah • mee • leh • yeem
I haven't had my period for...months.	**...aydan beri aybaşım olmuyor.** ...ie • _dahn_ beh • _ree_ _ie_ • bah • _shihm_ _ohl_ • moo • yohr

For Numbers, see page 20.

OPTICIAN

I've lost...	**...kaybettim.**
	...kie • beht • teem
a contact lens	**Bir kontak lensimi**
	beer kohn • tahk lehn • see • mee
my glasses	**Gözlüğümü**
	gurz • lyu • yu • myu
a lens	**Camımı**
	jah • mih • mih

PAYMENT & INSURANCE

How much?	**Ne kadar?**
	neh kah • dahr
Can I pay by credit card?	**Bu kredi kartı ile ödeme yapabilir miyim?**
	boo kreh • dee kahr • tih ee • leh
	ur • deh • meh yah • pah • bee • leer
	mee • yeem
I have insurance.	**Sigortam var.**
	see • gohr • tahm vahr
Can I have a receipt for my insurance?	**Sigorta için fiş alabilir miyim?**
	see • gohr • tah ee • cheen feesh
	ah • lah • bee • leer mee • yeem

PHARMACY

NEED TO KNOW

Where's the nearest pharmacy [chemist]?	**En yakın eczane nerede?** *ehn yah•kihn ehj•zah•neh neh•reh•deh*
What time does the pharmacy open/close [chemist]?	**Eczane ne zaman açılıyor/kapanıyor?** *ehj•zah•neh neh zah•mahn ah•chih•lih•yohr/kah•pah•nih•yohr*
What would you recommend for...?	**...için ne önerirdiniz?** *...ee•cheen neh ur•neh•reer•dee•neez*
How much should I take?	**Ne kadar almalıyım?** *neh kah•dahr ahl•mah•lih•yihm*
Can you fill [make up] this prescription for me?	**Bana bu reçeteyi hazırlar mısınız?** *bah•nah boo reh•cheh•teh•yee hah•zihr•lahr mih•sih•nihz*
I'm allergic to...	**...alerjim var.** *...ah•lehr•jeem vahr*

In Turkey, the **eczane** (pharmacy) fills medical prescriptions and sells non-prescription drugs as well as cosmetics. Regular hours are generally Monday to Saturday from 9:00 a.m. to 7:00 p.m. At other times, pharmacies work on a rotating schedule. Check the store window to find the closest **nöbetçi eczane** (all-night pharmacy).

WHAT TO TAKE

How much should I take? How often?	**Ne kadar almalıyım?** *neh kah • dahr ahl • mah • lih • yihm* **Günde kaç defa almalıyım?** *gyun • deh kahch deh • fah ahl • mah • lih • yihm*
Is it suitable for children? I'm taking…	**Çocuklar için uygun mu?** *choh • jook • lahr ee • cheen ooy • goon moo* **…alıyorum.** *…ah • lih • yoh • room*
Are there side effects? I'd like some medicine for…	**Yan etkisi var mı?** *yahn eht • kee • see vahr mih* **…için bir ilaç istiyorum.** *…ee • cheen beer ee • lahch ees • tee • yoh • room*
a cold	**Soğuk algınlığı** *soh • ook ahl • gihn • lih • ih*

YOU MAY SEE…

GÜNDE BİR/ÜÇ KERE	once/three times a day
TABLET	tablet
DAMLA	drop
ÇAY KAŞIĞI	teaspoon
YEMEKDEN ÖNCE	before meals
YEMEKDEN SONRA	after meals
YEMEKLERLE BİRLİKTE	with meals
AÇ KARNINA	on an empty stomach
BÜTÜN YUTUN	swallow whole
UYKUYA YOL AÇABILIR	may cause drowsiness
İÇİLMEZ	for external use only

a cough	**Öksürük**
	urk • syu • _ryuk_
diarrhea	**İshal**
	ees • _hahl_
a headache	**Baş ağrısı**
	bahs ah • rih • sih
insect bites	**Böcek sokması**
	bur • _jehk_ sohk • mah • _sih_
motion sickness	**Yol tutması**
	yohl toot • mah • _sih_
a sore throat	**Boğaz ağrısı**
	boh • _ahz_ ah • rih • sih
sunburn	**Güneş yanığı**
	gyu • _nehsh_ yah • nih • ih
a toothache	**Diş ağrısı**
	deesh ah • rih • sih
an upset stomach	**Mide bozukluğu**
	mee • _deh_ boh • zook • loo • oo

BASIC SUPPLIES

I'd like...	**...istiyorum.**
	...ees • _tee_ • yoh • room
acetaminophen [paracetamol]	**Parasetamol**
	pah • rah • _seh_ • tah • _mohl_
antiseptic cream	**Antiseptik krem**
	ahn • tee • sehp • _teek_ krehm
aspirin	**Aspirin**
	ahs • pee • _reen_
bandages [plasters]	**Bandaj**
	bahn • _dahj_
a comb	**Tarak**
	tah • _rahk_
condoms	**Prezervatif**
	preh • zehr • vah • _teef_

contact lens solution	**Kontakt lens solüsyonu**
	kohn • tahkt lehns soh • lyus • yoh • noo
deodorant	**Deodorant**
	deh • oh • doh • rahnt
a hairbrush	**Saç fırçası**
	sahch fihr • chah • sih
hair spray	**Saç spreyi**
	sahch spreh • yee
ibuprofen	**Ibuprofen**
	ee • boop • roh • fehn
insect repellent	**Böcek kovucu**
	bur • jek koh • voo • joo
a nail file	**Tırnak törpüsü**
	tihr • nahk turr • pyu • syu
a (disposable) razor	**(Tek kullanımlık) Jilet**
	(tehk kool • lah • nihm • lihk) jee • leht
razor blades	**Jilet**
	jee • leht
sanitary napkins [pads]	**Âdet bezi**
	ah • deht beh • zee
shampoo/ conditioner	**Şampuan/Saç kremi**
	shahm • poo • ahn/sahch kreh • mee
soap	**Sabun**
	sah • boon

sunscreen	**Güneş geçirmez krem**
	gyu • nehsh geh • cheer • mehz krehm
tampons	**Tampon**
	tahm • pohn
tissues	**Kağıt mendil**
	kah • iht mehn • deel
toilet paper	**Tuvalet kağıdı**
	too • vah • leht kah • ih • dih
a toothbrush	**Diş fırçası**
	deesh fihr • çah • sih
toothpaste	**Diş macunu**
	deesh mah • joo • noo

For Baby Essentials, see page 138.

CHILD HEALTH & EMERGENCY

Can you recommend a pediatrician?	**Bir çocuk doktoru önerir misiniz?**
	beer choh • jook dohk • toh • roo ur • neh • ree mee • see • neez
My child is allergic to...	**Çocuğumun...alerjisi var.**
	choh • joo • oo • moon...ah • lehr • jee • see vahr

My child is missing.	**Çocuğum kayıp.**
	choh • joo • <u>oom</u> kah • <u>yihp</u>
Have you seen a boy/girl?	**Bir oğlan/kız gördünüz mü?**
	beer oo • <u>lahn</u>/kihz gurr • dyu • <u>nyuz</u> myu

For Police, see page 146.

DISABLED TRAVELERS

NEED TO KNOW

Is there...?	**...var mı?**
	...vahr mih
access for the disabled	**Engelli girişi**
	ehn • gehl • <u>lee</u> gee • ree • <u>shee</u>
a wheelchair ramp	**Tekerlekli sandalye rampası**
	teh • kehr • lehk • <u>lee</u> sahn • <u>dahl</u> • yeh <u>rahm</u> • pah • sih
a handicapped [disabled-] accessible restroom [toilet]	**Özürlü tuvaleti**
	ur • zyur • <u>lyu</u> too • <u>vah</u> • leh • tee
I need...	**...ihtiyacım var.**
	...eeh • tee • yah • <u>jihm</u> vahr
assistance	**Yardımcıya**
	yahr • dihm • jih • <u>yah</u>
an elevator [lift]	**Asansöre**
	ah • sahn • sur • <u>reh</u>
a ground-floor room	**Zemin-kat odasına**
	zeh • <u>meen</u> • kaht oh • dah • sih • <u>nah</u>

ASKING FOR ASSISTANCE

I'm disabled.	**Ben özürlüyüm.**
	behn ur • zyur • lyu • yyum
I'm deaf.	**Ben sağırım.**
	behn sah • ih • rihm
I'm visually/hearing impaired.	**Görme/Duyma engelliyim.**
	gurr • meh/dooy • mah ehn • gel • lee • yeem
I'm unable to walk far.	**Uzağa yürüyemem.**
	oo • zah • ah yyu • ryu • yeh • mehm
I'm unable to use the steps.	**Merdivenleri kullanamam.** stairs.
	mehr • dee • vehn • leh • ree kool • lah • nah • mahm
Can I bring my wheelchair?	**Tekerlekli sandalyemi getirebilir miyim?**
	teh • kehr • lehk • lee sahn • dahl • yeh • mee geh • tee • reh • bee • leer mee • yeem
Are guide dogs permitted?	**Rehber köpeklere izin var mı?**
	reh • behr kur • pehk • leh • reh ee • zeen vah • mih

Can you help me?

Bana yardım edebilir misiniz?
bah • nah yahr • dihm eh • deh • bee • leer mee • see • neez

Please open/hold the door.

Lütfen kapıyı açın/tutun.
lyut • fehn kah • pih • yih ah • chihn/too • toon

FOOD & DRINK

EATING OUT   166
MEALS & COOKING   177
DRINKS   196
ON THE MENU   202

EATING OUT

NEED TO KNOW

Can you recommend good restaurant/bar?	**İyi bir lokanta/bar önerebilir misiniz?** ee • *yee* beer loh • *kahn* • tah/bahr ur • neh • reh • bee • *leer* mee • see • neez
Is there a traditional Turkish/an inexpensive restaurant near here?	**Yakınlarda geleneksel Türk yemekleri/ucuz yemek sunan bir lokanta var mı?** yah • kihn • lahr • *dah* geh • leh • *nehk* • sehl tyurk yeh • mehk • leh • *ree*/oo • *jooz* yeh • *mehk* soo • *nahn* beer loh • *kahn* • tah vahr mih
A table for…, please.	**…kişi için bir masa lütfen.** …kee • *shee* ee • cheen beer mah • *sah lyut* • fehn
Could we sit…?	**…oturabilir miyiz?** …oh • too • rah • bee • *leer* mee • yeez
here/there	**Burada/Orada** *boo* • rah • dah/*oh* • rah • dah
outside	**Dışarda** dih • shah • rih • *dah*
in a non-smoking area	**Sigara içilmeyen bir yerde** see • gah • *rah* ee • *cheel* • meh • yehn beer yehr • *deh*
I'm waiting for someone.	**Birini bekliyorum.** bee • ree • *nee* behk • lee • yoh • room
Where are the restrooms [toilets]?	**Tuvalet nerede?** too • vah • *leht neh* • reh • deh

A menu, please.	**Menü lütfen.**
	meh • nyu lyut • fehn
What do you recommend?	**Ne önerirsiniz?**
	neh ur • neh • reer • see • neez
I'd like…	**…istiyorum.**
	…ees • tee • yoh • room
Some more…, please.	**Biraz daha…istiyorum lütfen.**
	bee • rahz dah • hah…
	ees • tee • yoh • room lyut • fehn
Enjoy your meal.	**Afiyet olsun.**
	ah • fee • yeht ohl • soon
The check [bill], please.	**Hesap lütfen.**
	heh • sahp lyut • fehn
Is service included?	**Servis dahil mi?**
	sehr • vees dah • heel mee
Can I pay by credit card?	**Kredi kartı ile ödeme yapabilir miyim?**
	kreh • dee kahr • tih ee • leh
	ur • deh • meh yah • pah • bee • leer
	mee • yeem
Can I have a receipt please?	**Lütfen fiş alabilir miyim?**
	lyut • fehn feesh
	ah • lah • bee • leer mee • yeem
Thank you.	**Teşekkür ederim.**
	teh • shehk • kyur eh • deh • reem

WHERE TO EAT

Can you recommend…?	**…önerebilir misiniz?**
	…ur • neh • reh • bee • leer mee • see • neez
a restaurant	**Lokanta**
	loh • kahn • tah
a bar	**Bar**
	bahr

a cafe	**Kafe**
	kah • _feh_
a fast-food place	**Hazır yemek lokantası**
	hah • _zihr_ yeh • _mehk_ loh • _kahn_ • tah • sih
a cheap restaurant	**ucuz bir restoran**
	oo jooz beer res • _toh_ • rahn
an expensive restaurant	**pahalı bir restoran**
	pah • hah • lih beer res • _toh_ • rahn
a restaurant with a good view	**güzel manzaralı bir restoran**
	gyu • zehl mahn • zah • rah • lih beer res • _toh_ • rahn
an authentic/ a non-touristy restaurant	**otantik turistik olmayan bir restoran**
	oh • tahn • teek/too • rist • eek ohl • mah • yahn beer res • _toh_ • rahn

RESERVATIONS & PREFERENCES

I'd like to reserve a table…	**…bir masa ayırtmak istiyorum.**
	…beer mah • _sah_ ah • yihrt • _mahk_ ees • _tee_ • yoh • room
for two	**İki kişi için**
	ee • _kee_ kee • _shee_ ee • cheen
for this evening	**Bu gece**
	boo geh • jeh
for tomorrow at…	**Yarın saat…için**
	yah • _rihn_ sah • _aht_…ee • cheen
A table for two, please.	**İki kişilik bir masa lütfen.**
	ee • _kee_ kee • shee • _leek_ beer mah • _sah lyut_ • fehn
We have please. please.	**Yer ayırtmıştık.**
	yehr ah • yihrt • _mihsh_ • tihk
My name is…	**İsmim…**
	ees • _meem_…

Could we sit...?	**...oturabilir miyiz?**
	...oh • too • rah • bee • leer mee • yeez
here/there	**Burada/Orada**
	boo • rah • dah/oh • rah • dah
outside	**Dışarda**
	dih • shahr • dah
in a non-smoking area	**Sigara içilmeyen bir yerde**
	see • gah • rah ee • cheel • meh • yehn beer yehr • deh
by the window	**Pencere kenarında**
	pehn • jeh • reh keh • nah • rihn • dah

YOU MAY HEAR...

Rezervasyonunuz var mı?
reh • zehr • vah • syoh • noo • nooz vahr mih
Do you have a reservation?

Ne kadar?
neh kah • dahr
How many?

Sigara içilen bölümde mi içilmeyen bölümde mi?
see • gah • rah ee • chee • lehn bur • lyum • deh mee ee • cheel • meh • yehn bur • lyum • deh mee
Smoking or non-smoking?

Siparişinizi vermeye hazır mısınız?
see • pah • ree • shee • nee • zee vehr • meh • yeh hah • zihr mih • sih • nihz
Are you ready to order?

Ne istersiniz?
neh ees • tehr • see • neez
What would you like?

...öneririm.
...ur • neh • ree • reem
I recommend...

Afiyet olsun.
ah • fee • yeht ohl • soon
Enjoy your meal.

Where are the toilets?	**Tuvalet nerede?**
	too • vah • leht neh • reh • deh
Can I get a table in the shade/sun?	**Gölgede/güneşte bir masa alabilir miyim?**
	gurl • geh • deh/gyu • nash • teh beer
	mah • sah ah • lah • bee • leer mee • yeem

HOW TO ORDER

Waiter!/Waitress!	**Garson!**
	gahr • sohn
We're ready to order.	**Siparişleri verebiliriz.**
	see • pah • reesh • leh • ree
	veh • reh • bee • lee • reez
May I see the wine list, please?	**Şarap listesini görebilir miyim lütfen?**
	shah • rahp lees • teh • see • nee
	gur • reh • bee • leer mee • yeem lyut • fehn
I'd like…	**…istiyorum.**
	…ees • tee • yoh • room
a bottle of…	**Bir şişe…**
	beer shee • sheh…
a carafe of…	**Bir sürahi…**
	beer syu • rah • hee…
a glass of…	**Bir bardak…**
	beer bahr • dahk…

The menu, please.	**Menü lütfen.**
	meh • nyu lyut • fehn
Do you have...?	**...var mı?**
	...vahr mih
a menu in English	**İngilizce menü**
	een • gee • leez • jeh meh • nyu
a fixed-price menu	**Fiks menü**
	feeks meh • nyu
a children's menu	**Çocuk menüsü**
	choh • jook meh • nyu • syu lyut • fehn
What do you recommend?	**Ne önerirsiniz?**
	neh ur • neh • reer • see • neez
What's this?	**Bu nedir?**
	boo neh • deer
What's in it?	**İçinde ne var?**
	ee • cheen • deh neh vahr
Is it spicy?	**Baharatlı mı?**
	bah • hah • raht • lih mih
It's to go [take away].	**Paket olacak.**
	pah • keht oh • lah • jahk
I'd like...	**...istiyorum.**
	...ees • tee • yoh • room
More..., please.	**Daha...lütfen.**
	dah • hah...lyut • fehn
With/Without...	**...ile/-siz.**
	...ee • leh/ • seez
I can't have...	**...yiyemem.**
	...yee • yeh • mehm
I'd like...	**...istiyorum.**
	...ees • tee • yoh • room
rare	**az pişmiş**
	ahz peesh • meesh
medium	**orta ateşte**
	ohr • tah ah • tehsh • teh

| well-done | **iyi pişmiş** |
| | *ee • yee peesh • meesh* |

For Drinks, see page 196.

YOU MAY SEE...

MASA ÜCRETİ	cover charge
FİKS MENÜ	fixed-price
MENÜ	menu
GÜNÜN MENÜSÜ	menu of the day
HİZMET DAHİL (DEĞİL)	service (not) included
SPESİYALLER	specials

COOKING METHODS

baked	**fırında pişmiş**
	fih • rihn • dah peesh • meesh
boiled	**haşlanmış**
	hash • lahn • mihsh
braised	**hafif ateşte pişmiş**
	hah • feef ah • tesh • teh peesh • meesh
breaded	**ekmek kırıntıları ile kızartılmış**
	ehk • mehk kih • rihn • tih • lah • rih ee • leh
	kih • zahr • tihl • mihsh
creamed	**kremalı**
	kreh • mah • lih
diced	**kuşbaşı doğranmış**
	koosh • bah • shih doh • rahn • mihsh
filleted	**filetolanmış**
	fee • leh • toh • lahn • mihsh
fried	**kızartma**
	kih • zahrt • mah

grilled	**ızgara**
	ihz • gah • <u>rah</u>
poached	**haşlama**
	hahsh • lah • <u>mah</u>
roasted	**kızarmış**
	kih • zahr • <u>mihsh</u>
sautéed	**sote**
	soh • <u>teh</u>
smoked	**tütsülenmiş**
	tyut • syu • lehn • <u>meesh</u>
steamed	**buğulama**
	boo • oo • lah • <u>mah</u>
stewed	**yahni**
	yah • <u>hnee</u>
stuffed	**dolma**
	dohl • <u>mah</u>

DIETARY REQUIREMENTS

I'm...	**Ben...**
	behn...
diabetic	**şeker hastasıyım**
	sheh • <u>kehr</u> hahs • tah • <u>sih</u> • yihm

lactose intolerant	**laktoza duyarlıyım**
	lahk • toh • zah doo • yahr • lih • yihm
vegetarian	**vejetaryenim**
	veh • jeh • tahr • yeh • neem
vegan	**vejeteryan**
	veh • zheh • tehr • yahn
I'm allergic to…	**…ya alerjim var.**
	…yah ahl • lehr • jeem vahr
I can't eat…	**…içeren yiyecek yiyemem.** …
	ee • cheh • rehn yee • yeh • jehk
	yee • yeh • mehm
dairy	**Süt ürünleri**
	syut yu • ryun • leh • ree
gluten	**Glüten**
	glyu • tehn
nuts	**Kuruyemiş**
	koo • roo • yeh • meesh
pork	**Domuz eti**
	doh • mooz eh • tee
shellfish	**Kabuklu deniz ürünleri**
	kah • book • loo deh • neez
	yu • ryun • leh • ree
spicy foods	**Baharatlı yiyecekler**
	bah • hah • raht • lih yee • yeh • jehk • lehr
wheat	**Hamur işleri**
	hah • moor eesh • leh • ree
Is it halal/kosher?	**Helal/Kaşer mi?**
	heh • lahl/kah • shehr mee
Do you have…?	**…var mı?**
	…vahr mih
skimmed milk	**yağsız süt**
	yah • sihz syut
whole milk	**tam yağlı süt**
	tahm yah • lih syut
soya milk	**soya sütü**
	soh • yah syu • tyu

DINING WITH CHILDREN

Do you have children's portions?
Çocuk porsiyonunuz var mı?
choh • jook pohr • see • yoh • noo • nooz vahr mih

A highchair/child's seat, please.
Yüksek sandalye/Çocuk sandalyesi lütfen.
yuk • sehk sahn • dahl • yeh/choh • jook sahn • dahl • yeh • see lyut • fehn

Where can I feed/ change the baby?
Bebeği nerede besleyebilirim/üstünü değiştirebilirim?
beh • beh • yee neh • reh • deh behs • leh • yeh • bee • lee • reem/ yus • tyu • nyu deh • yeesh • tee • reh • bee • lee • reem

Can you warm this?
Bunu ısıtabilir misiniz?
boo • noo ih • sih • tah • bee • leer mee • see • neez

For Traveling with Children, see page 137.

HOW TO COMPLAIN

How much longer will our food be?
Yemek için daha ne kadar bekleyeceğiz?
yeh • mehk ee • cheen dah • hah neh kah • dahr behk • leh • yeh • jeh • yeez

We can't wait any longer.
Daha fazla bekleyemeyeceğiz.
dah • hah fahz • lah behk • leh • yeh • meh • yeh • jeh • yeez

We're leaving.
Gidiyoruz.
gee • dee • yoh • rooz

This isn't clean/fresh.
Bu temiz/taze değil.
boo teh • meez/tah • zeh deh • yeel

I can't eat this.
Bunu yiyemem.
boo • noo yee • yeh • mehm

This is too…	**Bu çok…**
	boo <u>chohk</u>…
cold/hot	**soğuk/sıcak**
	soh • <u>ook</u>/sih • jahk
salty/spicy	**tuzlu/baharatlı**
	tooz • <u>loo</u>/bah • hah • raht • <u>lih</u>
tough/bland	**sert/yumuşak**
	sehrt/yoo • moo • <u>shahk</u>
I didn't order this.	**Benim siparişim bu değil.**
	beh • <u>neem</u> see • pah • ree • <u>sheem</u> boo
	<u>deh</u> • yeel
I ordered…	**…söyledim.**
	…sur • yleh • <u>deem</u>

PAYING

The check [bill], please.	**Hesap lütfen.**
	heh • <u>sahp</u> lyut • fehn
We'd like to pay separately.	**Ayrı ayrı ödemek istiyoruz.**
	ie • <u>rih</u> ie • <u>rih</u> ur • deh • <u>mehk</u>
	ees • <u>tee</u> • yoh • rooz
It's all together.	**Hepsi birlikte lütfen.**
	hehp • see beer • leek • teh lyut • fehn
Is service included?	**Servis dahil mi?**
	sehr • <u>vees</u> dah • <u>heel</u> mee
What's this amount for?	**Bu miktar ne için?**
	boo meek • <u>tahr</u> neh ee • cheen
I didn't have that. I had…	**Bunu almadım. …aldım.**
	boo • <u>noo ahl</u> • mah • dihm…ahl • <u>dihm</u>
Can I pay by credit card?	**Kredi kartı ile ödeme yapabilir miyim?**
	kreh • <u>dee</u> kahr • <u>tih</u> ee • leh
	ur • deh • <u>meh</u> yah • pah • bee • <u>leer</u>
	mee • yeem

an I have an emized bill/ receipt?	**Dökümlü hesap/Fiş alabilir miyim?** dur • kyum • lyu heh • sahp/feesh ah • lah • bee • leer mee • yeem
at was a very good eal.	**Yemek çok güzeldi.** yeh • mehk chohk gyu • zehl • dee
e already paid	**Zaten ödedim.** zah • tehn ur • deh • deem

r Numbers, see page 20.

Service is included in the price at cafes and restaurants. However, people do tend to leave a small tip. Round up the bill to the nearest euro or two for good service.

MEALS & COOKING

Meze (appetizers) are the perfect accompaniment to a leisurely drink before dinner. **Meze** may be hot, **sıcak mezeler** (hot appetizers), or cold, **soğuk mezeler** (cold appetizers). The selection that is served usually depends on the main course to follow. Dried or marinated mackerel, vegetables cooked in oil, tomato and cucumber salad or deep fried mussels and calamari in sauce may precede grilled fish or meat. Hummus, marinated stuffed eggplant, lentil balls or spicy peppers with nuts might be served before a main dish of kebab.

BREAKFAST

bal	honey
bahl	
ekmek	bread
ehk • mehk	
greyfurt	grapefruit
gray • foort	
küçük yuvarlak ekmek	rolls
kyu • chyuk yoo • vahr • lahk ehk • mehk	
kızarmış ekmek	roasted bread
kih • zahr • mihsh ehk • mehk	
marmelat	marmalade
mahr • meh • laht	
meyve suyu	fruit juice
may • veh soo • yoo	
portakal	orange
pohr • tah • kahl	
reçel	jam
reh • chehl	
süt	milk
syut	
tereyağı	butter
teh • reh • yah • ih	
...yumurta	...eggs
...yoo • moor • tah	

çırpma	scrambled
chihrp • mah	
katı	boiled
kah • tih	
sahanda	fried
sah • hahn • dah	

APPETIZERS

rnavut ciğeri	fried liver morsels
hr • nah • voot jee • yeh • ree	
eyaz peynir	white cheese
eh • yahz pay • neer	
örek	hot filo pastries
ur • rehk	
olma	stuffed grape leaves
ohl • mah	
nam bayıldı	stuffed eggplant [aubergine]
e • mahm bah • yihl • dih	
atlıcan salatası	eggplant [aubergine] salad
aht • lih • jahn sah • lah • tah • sih	
ilaki	beans in olive oil
ee • lah • kee	
arama	fish roe pâté
ıh • rah • mah	

SOUP

balık çorbası
bah • lihk chohr • bah • sih

et suyuna çorba
eht soo • yoo • nah chohr • bah

kremalı çorba
kreh • mah • lih chohr • bah

patates çorbası
pah • tah • tehs chohr • bah • sih

sebze çorbası
sehb • zeh chohr • bah • sih

soğan çorbası
soh • ahn chohr • bah • sih

tavuk çorbası
tah • vook chohr • bah • sih

fish soup

consommé

cream soup

potato soup

vegetable soup

onion soup

chicken soup

FISH & SEAFOOD

ahtapot
ah • tah • poht

alabalık
ah • lah • bah • lihk

octopus

trout

deniz tarağı	clams
deh • _neez_ tah • rah • ih	
ıstakoz	lobster
ihs • tah • _kohz_	
istiridye	oysters
ees • tee • _reed_ • yeh	
kalamar	squid
kah • lah • _mahr_	
karides	shrimp [prawns]
kah • ree • _dehs_	
lüfer	bluefish
yu • _fehr_	
midye	mussels
meed • _yeh_	
morina balığı	cod
moh • _ree_ • nah bah • lih • _ih_	
pisi balığı	plaice
ee • _see_ bah • lih • _ih_	
ringa balığı	herring [whitebait]
reen • _gah_ bah • lih • _ih_	
ton balığı	tuna
ohn bah • lih • _ih_	

kılıç şiş
kih • lihch sheesh

swordfish kebabs grilled with bay leaves, tomatoes and green peppers

Çınarcık usulü balık
chih • nahr • jihk oo • soo • lyu bah • lihk

fried swordfish, sea bass and shrimp, served with mushrooms

uskumru pilakisi
oos • koom • roo pee • lah • kee • see

mackerel fried in olive oil, with potatoes, celery, carrots and garlic; served cold

MEAT & POULTRY

bonfile
bohn • fee • leh

steak

böbrek
bur • brehk

kidneys

but
boot

leg

but eti
boot eh • tee

rump

ciğer
jee • ehr

liver

Çerkez tavuğu
chehr • kehz tah • voo • oo

Circassian chicken: boiled chicken with rice and nut sauce

çiğ köfte
chee kurf • teh

raw meatballs made from ground meat and cracked wheat

dana
dah • nah

veal

omuz oh • <u>mooz</u>	pork
ana pirzolası ah • <u>nah</u> peer • zoh • lah • sih	T-bone steak
eto e • <u>leh</u> • toh	fillet
ndi een • <u>dee</u>	turkey
mbon hm • <u>bohn</u>	ham
emikli et h • meek • <u>lee</u> eht	cutlet
zu o • <u>zoo</u>	lamb
zu dolması o • <u>zoo</u> dohl • mah • <u>sih</u>	lamb stuffed with savory rice, liver and pistachios
zu güveç o • <u>zoo</u> gyu • <u>vehch</u>	lamb stew with onions, garlic, potatoes, tomatoes and herbs
dek • <u>rdehk</u>	duck

pirzola	chops
peer • zoh • lah	
sığır eti	beef
sih • ihr eh • tee	
sığır filetosu	sirloin
sih • ihr fee • leh • toh • soo	
sosis	sausages
soh • sees	
sülün	pheasant
syu • lyun	
şiş köfte	ground lamb croquettes on a skewer, grilled over charcoal
sheesh kurf • teh	
tavuk	chicken
tah • vook	
tavşan	rabbit
tahv • shahn	
yoğurtlu kebab	kebab on toasted bread with pureed tomatoes and seasoned yogurt
yoh • oort • loo keh • bahb	

ⓘ

Turkish cuisine is complex, reflecting Turkey's situation as a crossroads where East meets West. You'll find there is a healthy emphasis on fresh meat, fish and vegetables mixed with spices. **Şiş kebab** (skewered cubes of meat) and **baklava** (filo pastry stuffed with honey and pistachio nuts) are two typical Turkish dishes known and enjoyed around the world.

VEGETABLES & STAPLES

ezelye *eh • zehl • yeh*	peas
ber *e • behr*	peppers
mates *h • mah • tehs*	tomatoes
vuç *h • vooch*	carrots
ar *h • yahr*	cucumber
bak *h • bahk*	zucchini [courgette]
reviz *h • reh • veez*	celery
ana *h • hah • nah*	cabbage
ntar *hn • tahr*	mushrooms
rul *h • rool*	lettuce
tates *h • tah • tehs*	potatoes

patlıcan *paht • lih • jahn*	eggplant [aubergine]
pirinç *pee • reench*	rice
sarı şalgam *sah • rih shahl • gahm*	rutabaga [swede]
sarmısak *sahr • mih • sahk*	garlic
soğan *soh • ahn*	onions
şalgam *shahl • gahm*	turnips
taze fasulye *tah • zeh fah • sool • yeh*	green beans
taze soğan *tah • zeh soh • ahn*	shallots [spring onions]
dere otu *deh • reh oh • too*	dill
karanfil *kah • rahn • feel*	cloves
kekik *keh • keek*	thyme
kırmızı biber *kihr • mih • zih bee • behr*	chili

kimyon keem • _yohn_	cumin
kişniş keesh • _neesh_	cilantro
maydanoz mie • dah • _nohz_	parsley
nane nah • _neh_	mint
safran sahf • _rahn_	saffron

(i)

Dolma is the term for any stuffed vegetable. Stuffing may be made of a mix of ground meat, cheese, onion and tomato or may be a vegetarian rice stuffing with tomato, onion and garlic. Meat-filled **dolma** are usually served as a main course dish with yogurt sauce, while rice-filled **dolma** are usually cooked in olive oil and eaten at room temperature.

FRUIT

ahududu *ah • hoo • doo • <u>doo</u>*	raspberries
çilek *chee • <u>lehk</u>*	strawberries
elma *ehl • <u>mah</u>*	apples
erik *eh • <u>reek</u>*	plums
greyfurt *gray • <u>foort</u>*	grapefruit
karpuz *kahr • <u>pooz</u>*	watermelon
kavun *kah • <u>voon</u>*	melon
kiraz *kee • <u>rahz</u>*	cherries
muz *mooz*	bananas
nar *nahr*	pomegranates
portakal *pohr • tah • <u>kahl</u>*	oranges

ftali	peaches
ehf • tah • lee	
üm	grapes
• zyum	

CHEESE

yaz peynir	white cheese
h • yahz pay • neer	
şar	hard cheese
h • shahr	
lu peynir	herb cheese
t • loo pay • neer	
lum peyniri	goat cheese
• loom pay • nee • ree	

DESSERT

(i)

The most common dessert after a meal is fresh seasonal fruit, though Turkish cooking offers a whole range of delights to try. Puddings, known as **muhallebi**, may or may not be milk-based and may be mixed with a variety of ingredients such as citrus fruit or even very thin slices of chicken breast. **Lokma** (dessert of fried dough dipped in syrup) and **helva** (sauteed flour and pine nuts mixed with milk and sugar or water) are also traditional desserts. The internationally-famous **baklava** (filo pastry stuffed with honey and pistachio nuts) is commonly eaten with coffee or after a kebab dish and the also well-known **lokum** (Turkish delight) is eaten as a digestive after meals.

aşure ah • <u>shoo</u> • reh	sweet, cold soup made of mixed grains, beans and dried fruits
ayva tatlısı ie • <u>vah</u> taht • lih • sih	baked quince slices in a syrup
baklava <u>bahk</u> • lah • vah	filo pastry filled with honey and pistachio nuts
kabak tatlısı kah • <u>bahk</u> taht • lih • sih	baked pumpkin in a syrup
kadayıf kah • <u>dah</u> • yihf	shredded wheat dessert, similar to baklava
kazandibi kah • <u>zahn</u> • dee • bee	oven-browned milk pudding
muhallebi moo • <u>hahl</u> • leh • bee	milk pudding
sütlaç syut • <u>lahch</u>	rice pudding
tavuk göğsü tah • <u>vook</u> gur • hsyu	milk pudding with thin filaments of chicken breast

SAUCES & CONDIMENTS

salt	**tuz** tooz
pepper	**karabiber** kah • rah • bee • be
mustard	**hardal** hahr • dahl
ketchup	**ketçap** keht • chahp

AT THE MARKET

In Turkey, there are a number of large supermarket and discount chains to shop in. They feature both local products as well as imported food. **Bakkal** (local grocery stores) can be found on just about every city block and offer enough to fill basic needs. There are also numerous specialty options: **çarşı** (small fruit and vegetable market), **balıkçı** (the fish store), and **kasap** (the butcher), in addition to the weekly **pazar** (neighborhood markets). In Istanbul be sure to visit the **Kapalı Çarşı** (covered bazaar) and the **Mısır Çarşısı** (spice bazaar).

YOU MAY HEAR...

Yardımcı olabilir miyim?
yahr • dihm • jih oh • lah • bee • leer mee • yeem

Can I help you?

Ne istersiniz?
neh ees • tehr • see • neez

What would you like?

Başka bir şey?
bahsh • kah beer shay

Anything else?

...lira.
...lee • rah

That's...lira.

here are the carts [trolleys]/baskets?	**El arabaları/Sepetler nerede?** *ehl ah • rah • bah • lah • rih/seh • peht • lehr neh • reh • deh*
here is...?	**...nerede?** *...neh • reh • deh*

I'd like some of that/those.	**Şundan/Şunlardan biraz istiyorum.** *shoon • dahn/shoon • lahr • dahn beer • ahz ees • tee • yoh • room*
Can I taste it?	**Tadına bakabilir miyim?** *tah • dih • nah bah • kah • bee • leer mee • yeem*
May I have…?	**…alabilir miyim?** *…ah • lah • bee • leer mee • yeem*
a kilo/half-kilo of…	**…dan bir/yarım kilo** *…dahn beer/yah • rihm kee • loh*
a liter/half-liter of…	**…dan bir/yarım litre** *…dahn beer/yah • rihm lee • treh*
a piece of…	**…bir parça** *…beer pahr • chah*
a slice of…	**…bir dilim** *…beer dee • leem*
More/Less.	**Daha fazla/az.** *dah • hah fahz • lah/ahz*
How much?	**Ne kadar?** *neh kah • dahr*
Where do I pay?	**Nereye ödeyeceğim?** *neh • reh • yeh ur • deh • yeh • jeh • yeem*

ay I have a bag?	**Bir çanta, alabilir miyim?**
	beer chahn • tah ah • lah • bee • leer
	mee • yeem
a being helped.	**Yardım alıyorum.**
	yahr • dihm ah • lih • yoh • room

Money, see page 30.

(i)

Measurements in Turkey are metric – and that
applies to the weight of food too. If you tend to think
n pounds and ounces, it's worth brushing up on what the
metric equivalent is before you go shopping for fruit and veg
n markets and supermarkets. Five hundred grams, or half a
kilo, is a common quantity to order, and that converts to just
over a pound (17.65 ounces, to be precise).

(eye icon)

YOU MAY SEE...

SON KULLANMA TARİHİ...	expiration date...
KALORİ	calories
YAĞSIZ	fat free
BUZDOLABINDA SAKLAYINIZ	keep refrigerated
...UFAK BİR MİKTARINI ÇEREBİLİR	may contain small traces of...
EN GEÇ...TARİHİNE KADAR SATILABİLİR	may be sold until...
VEJETARYENLER İÇİN UYGUNDUR	suitable for vegetarians

IN THE KITCHEN

bottle opener	**şişe açacağı**
	shee • _sheh_ ah • chah • jah • _ih_
bowls	**çanak**
	chah • _nahk_
can opener	**konserve açacağı**
	kon • sehr • _veh_ ah • chah • jah • _ih_
corkscrew	**şarap açacağı**
	shah • _rahp_ ah • chah • jah • _ih_
cups	**fincan**
	fihn • _jahn_
forks	**çatal**
	chah • _tahl_
frying pan	**tava**
	tah • _vah_
glasses	**bardak**
	bahr • _dahk_
knives	**bıçak**
	bih • _chahk_
measuring cup/	**ölçü kabı/kaşığı**
spoon	url • _chyu_ kah • _bih_/kah • shih • _ih_
napkin	**kağıt peçete**
	kah • _iht_ peh • _cheh_ • teh

...tes	**tabak**
	tah • <u>bakh</u>
...t	**çömlek**
	churm • <u>lehk</u>
...ucepan	**tencere**
	tehn • <u>jeh</u> • reh
...atula	**spatula**
	spah • <u>too</u> • lah
...oons	**kaşık**
	kah • <u>shihk</u>

Domestic Items, see page 81.

DRINKS

NEED TO KNOW

May I see the wine list/drink menu, please?	**Şarap listesini/İçecek menüsünü görebilir miyim lütfen?** *shah • rahp lees • teh • see • nee/ ee • cheh • jehk meh • nyu • syu • nyu gur • reh • bee • leer mee • yeem lyut • fehn*
What do you recommend?	**Ne önerirsiniz?** *neh ur • neh • reer • see • neez*
I'd like a bottle/ glass of red/ white wine.	**Bir şişe/bardak kırmızı/beyaz şarap istiyorum.** *beer shee • sheh/bahr • dahk kihr • mih • zih/beh • yahz shah • rahp ees • tee • yoh • room*
The house wine, please.	**Ev şarabı lütfen.** *ehv shah • rah • bih lyut • fehn*
Another bottle/ glass, please.	**Bir şişe/bardak daha lütfen.** *beer shee • sheh/bahr • dahk dah • hah lyut • fehn*
May I have a local beer?	**Yerel bir bira alabilir miyim?** *yeh • rehl beer bee • rah ah • lah • bee • leer mee • yeem*
Let me buy you a drink.	**Size bir içki ısmarlayayım.** *see • zeh beer eech • kee ihs • mahr • lah • yah • yihm*
Cheers!	**Şerefe!** *sheh • reh • feh*
A coffee/tea, please. Black.	**Kahve/Çay lütfen.** *kah • hveh/chie lyut • fehn* **Sütsüz.** *syut • syuz*

With milk.	**Sütlü.**
	syut • lyu
With sugar.	**Şekerli.**
	sheh • kehr • lee
With artificial sweetener.	**Yapay tatlandırıcılı.**
	yah • pie taht • lahn • dih • rih • jih • lih
...please.	**...lütfen.**
	...lyut • fehn
Fruit juice	**Meyve suyu**
	may • veh soo • yoo
Soda	**Soda**
	soh • dah
Sparkling/still water	**Maden/Sade su**
	mah • dehn/sah • deh soo
Is the tap water safe to drink?	**Musluk suyu içilir mi?**
	moos • look soo • yoo ee • chee • leer mee

A number of non-alcoholic drinks are available in Turkey. Soft drinks and mineral water are easily found, though you may choose to enjoy a freshly-squeezed fruit juice, particularly in winter when citrus fruit is in season. And though Turkish coffee is internationally known, tea is more commonly drunk throughout the day. Black tea and herbal infusions are typical. Traditional drinks include **ayran** (yogurt drink), **boza** (fermented millet drink) and **sahlep** (wild orchid drink). **Ayran** is made by diluting yogurt and is often served with a pinch of salt added; it is a particularly refreshing drink in the summer. **Boza** and **sahlep** are only served in winter. **Boza** has a flavor similar to eggnog and **sahlep**, made from pulverized wild orchid roots, is sweet and is usually served with cinnamon sprinkled on top.

NON-ALCOHOLIC DRINKS

ayran *ie • rahn*	natural yogurt drink
kola *koh • lah*	soda
limonata *lee • moh • nah • tah*	lemonade
çay *chie*	tea
...kahve *...kah • hveh*	coffee...
kafeini alınmış *kah • feh • ee • nee ah • lihn • mihsh*	decaffeinated
sütlü *syut • lyu*	with milk
sütsüz *syut • syuz*	black
gazlı/gazsız maden suyu *gahz • lih/gahz • sihz mah • dehn soo • yoo*	sparkling/still mineral water
salep *sah • lehp*	hot herbal drink
...suyu *...soo • yoo*	...juice

ananas	pineapple
ah • nah • nahs	
domates	tomato
doh • mah • tehs	
portakal	orange
pohr • tah • kahl	
...it	milk
...ut	
...tlü meyve suyu	milk shake
...ut • lyu may • veh soo • yoo	
...lgam suyu	turnip juice
...ahl • gahm soo • yoo	

YOU MAY HEAR...

Size bir içki alabilir miyim?	Can I get you a drink?
see • zeh beer eech • kee ah • lah • bee • leer mee • yeem	
Sütlü/Şekerli?	With milk/ sugar?
syut • lyu/sheh • kehr • lee	
Gazlı/Gazsız su?	Sparkling/Still water?
gahz • lih/gahz • sihz soo	

APERITIFS, COCKTAILS & LIQUEURS

...n	gin
...en	
...ikli konyak	plum brandy, slivovitz
...h • reek • lee kohn • yahk	
...ayısılı konyak	apricot brandy
...ah • yih • sih • lih kohn • yahk	
...onyak	brandy
...ohn • yahk	

Foreign spirits are available in Turkey, but the national drink is **raki** (aniseed liquor). Nearly 90-proof, it is usually drunk with a bit of added water. Adding water turns it a milky-white, which has earned the drink the nickname 'lion's milk.' Besides **raki**, Turkey also produces very good brands of dry red and white wine and a few types of beer, of which Efes is the most common.

viski
vees • kee
whisky

votka
voht • kah
vodka

BEER

bira
bee • rah
beer

fıçı
fih • chih
draft [draught]

şişe
shee • sheh
bottled

WINE

beyaz şarap
beh • yahz shah • rahp
white wine

kırmızı şarap
kihr • mih • zih shah • rahp
red wine

köpüklü şarap
kur • pyuk • lyu shah • rahp
sparkling wine

pembe şarap
pem • beh shah • rahp
blush [rosé] wine

sek şarap	dry wine
sehk shah • *rahp*	
tatlı şarap	sweet wine
taht • lih shah • *rahp*	

ℹ️

A number of grape varieties are grown in Turkey and the country has a long history of wine production. Each region specializes in a few particular types of wine, depending on the grapes that are grown there, so ask to try a local wine.

ℹ️

There are several different denominations of eating and drinking establishments in Turkey. **Restoran** (restaurant) used to be a term reserved only for the finest establishments, but now many different types of places use the name. **Lokanta** (family-run restaurants) are more economical and unpretentious. The food in **lokanta** is generally prepared in advance rather than to order and is often served cafeteria-style. **Meyhane** (taverns) are generally smoke-filled, noisy taverns that serve wine, **rakı** (aniseed liquor) and **meze** (appetizers), while **birahane** (beer hall) are typical beer halls. **Kebapci** (kebab joint), **dönerci** (doner joint) and **pideci** (a place specializing in **pide**, Turkish-style pizza) are the Turkish equivalents of fast-food places.

Keep in mind that not all restaurants will present you with a menu upon sitting down, but may instead offer you something seasonal or the specialty of the house or may just begin bringing **meze** (appetizers). In many establishments a tray is brought and you can select what you would like. Know that you are not obligated to accept every plate the waiter brings. Though many people choose to make an entire meal out of **meze** (appetizers), if you'd like to try some of the delicious main dish options, don't forget to save some room! Remember that fish is also sold by weight, so feel free to request that the waiter weigh it beforehand.

ON THE MENU

ahtapot
ah • tah • <u>poht</u>

octopus

ahududu
ah • hoo • doo • <u>doo</u>

raspberry

alabalık
ah • <u>lah</u> • bah • <u>lihk</u>

trout

ananas
ah • nah • <u>nahs</u>

pineapple

arnavut ciğeri
ahr • nah • <u>voot</u> jee • yeh • <u>ree</u>

fried liver morsels

aşure
ah • <u>shoo</u> • reh

sweet, cold soup
made of mixed
grains, beans and
dried fruits

ayran
ie • <u>rahn</u>

natural yogurt drink

ayva tatlısı
ie • <u>vah</u> taht • lih • sih

baked quince slices
in a syrup

az pişmiş
<u>ahz</u> peesh • meesh

rare

baklava
<u>bahk</u> • lah • vah

filo pastry filled with
honey and pistachio
nuts

bal
bahl

honey

balık çorbası
bah • <u>lihk</u> chohr • bah • sih

fish soup

beyaz peynir
beh • <u>yahz</u> pay • neer

white cheese

beyaz şarap
beh • <u>yahz</u> shah • rahp

white wine

bezelye
beh • <u>zehl</u> • yeh

peas

ber	pepper
ee • behr	
ra	beer
ee • rah	
nfile	steak
ohn • fee • leh	
oza	a calorie-packed,
oh • zah	sour-tasting drink
	made from
	fermented millet
öbrek	kidney
ur • brehk	
örek	hot filo pastries
ur • rehk	
ut	leg
oot	
ut eti	rump
oot eh • tee	
ğer	liver
e • ehr	
n	gin
en	
ay	tea
nie	

Çerkez tavuğu
chehr • kehz tah • voo • oo

Circassian chicken: boiled chicken with rice and nut sauce

Çınarcık usulü balık
chih • nahr • jihk oo • soo • lyu bah • lihk

fried swordfish, sea bass and shrimp, served with mushrooms

çırpma
chihrp • mah

scrambled

çiğ köfte
chee kurf • teh

raw meatballs made from ground meat and cracked wheat

çilek
chee • lehk

strawberry

dana
dah • nah

veal

dana pirzolası
dah • nah peer • zoh • lah • sih

T-bone steak

deniz tarağı
deh • neez tah • rah • ih

clams

dere otu
deh • reh oh • too

dill

dolma
dohl • mah

stuffed grape leaves

domates
doh • mah • tehs

tomato

domuz
doh • mooz

pork

ekmek
ehk • mehk

bread

elma
ehl • mah

apple

erik
eh • reek

plum

kli konyak • reek • *lee* kohn • *yahk*	plum brandy, slivovitz
uyuna çorba soo • yoo • *nah* chohr • *bah*	consommé
şarabı shah • rah • bih	house wine
chih	draft [draught]
to • *leh* • toh	fillet
lı z • *lih*	sparkling water
lı maden suyu z • *lih* mah • *dehn* soo • yoo	sparkling mineral water
sız z • *sihz*	still water
sız maden suyu z • *sihz* mah • *dehn* soo • yoo	still mineral water
yfurt y • *foort*	grapefruit
uç • *vooch*	carrot
ar • *yahr*	cucumber

hindi *heen • dee*	turkey
ıstakoz *ihs • tah • kohz*	lobster
içecek menüsünü *ee • cheh • jehk meh • nyu • syu*	drink menu
içki *eech • kee*	drink
imam bayıldı *ee • mahm bah • yihl • dih*	eggplant [aubergine] stuffed with tomato and cooked in olive oil
istiridye *ees • tee • reed • yeh*	oysters
iyi pişmiş *ee • yee peesh • meesh*	well-done
jambon *jahm • bohn*	ham
kabak *kah • bahk*	zucchini [courgette]
kabak musakkası *kah • bahk moo • sahk • kah • sih*	sautéed and fried eggplant [aubergine] green peppers, tomatoes, onions, zucchini [courgette] and ground meat
kabak tatlısı *kah • bahk taht • lih • sih*	baked pumpkin in a syrup
kadayıf *kah • dah • yihf*	shredded wheat dessert, similar to baklava
kafeini alınmış *kah • feh • ee • nee ah • lihn • mihsh*	decaffeinated
kahve *kah • hveh*	coffee

kalamar	squid
kah • lah • _mahr_	
karanfil	cloves
kah • rahn • _feel_	
karides	shrimp [prawn]
kah • ree • _dehs_	
karpuz	watermelon
kahr • _pooz_	
kaşar	hard cheese
kah • _shahr_	
katı	boiled
kah • _tih_	
kavun	melon
kah • _voon_	
kayısılı konyak	apricot brandy
kah • yih • sih • _lih_ kohn • _yahk_	
kazandibi	oven-browned milk
kah • _zahn_ • dee • bee	pudding
kekik	thyme
keh • _keek_	
kemikli et	cutlet
keh • meek • _lee_ eht	

kereviz	celery
keh • reh • veez	
kılıç şiş	swordfish kebab grilled with bay leaves, tomatoes and green peppers
kih • lihch sheesh	
kırmızı biber	chili
kih • mih • zih bee • behr	
kırmızı şarap	red wine
kihr • mih • zih shah • rahp	
kızarmış ekmek	roasted bread
kih • zahr • mihsh ehk • mehk	
kimyon	cumin
keem • yohn	
kiraz	cherry
kee • rahz	
kişniş	cilantro
keesh • neesh	
kola	soda
koh • lah	
konyak	brandy (cognac)
kohn • yahk	
köpüklü şarap	sparkling wine
kyu • pyuk • lyu shah • rahp	

köpüksüz şarap	still wine
kyu • pyuk • _syuz_ shah • _rahp_	
kremalı çorba	cream soup
kreh • mah • _lih_ chohr • _bah_	
kuzu	lamb
koo • _zoo_	
kuzu dolması	lamb stuffed with
koo • _zoo_ dohl • mah • _sih_	savory rice, liver and
	pistachios
kuzu güveç	lamb stew with
koo • _zoo_ gyu • _vehch_	onions, garlic,
	potatoes, tomatoes
	and herbs
küçük yuvarlak ekmek	bread rolls
kyu • _chyuk_ yoo • vahr • _lahk_ ehk • _mehk_	
ahana	cabbage
ah • _hah_ • nah	
eblebi	roasted chick peas
ehb • leh • _bee_	
imonata	lemonade
ee • moh • _nah_ • tah	
okum	Turkish delight
oh • _koom_	

lüfer	bluefish
lyu • <u>fehr</u>	
mantar	mushroom
mahn • <u>tahr</u>	
marmelat	marmalade
mahr • meh • <u>laht</u>	
marul	lettuce
mah • <u>rool</u>	
maydanoz	parsley
mie • dah • <u>nohz</u>	
meyve suyu	fruit juice
may • <u>veh</u> soo • yoo	
meze	appetizers
meh • <u>zeh</u>	
midye	mussels
meed • <u>yeh</u>	
morina balığı	cod
moh • <u>ree</u> • nah bah • lih • <u>ih</u>	
muhallebi	milk pudding
moo • <u>hahl</u> • leh • bee	
muz	banana
mooz	
nane	mint
nah • <u>neh</u>	

ar	pomegranate
ahr	
rta ateşte	medium
hr • tah ah • tehsh • teh	
tlu peynir	herb cheese
ht • loo pay • neer	
rdek	duck
r • rdehk	
atates	potato
ah • tah • tehs	
atates çorbası	potato soup
ah • tah • tehs chohr • bah • sih	
atlıcan	eggplant [aubergine]
aht • lih • jahn	
atlıcan salatası	eggplant [aubergine] salad
ath • lih • jahn sah • lah • tah • sih	
embe şarap	blush [rosé] wine
em • beh shah • rahp	
ilaki	beans in olive oil
ee • lah • kee	
irinç	rice
ee • reench	
irzola	chops
eer • zoh • lah	

pisi balığı *pee • see bah • lih • ih*	plaice
portakal *pohr • tah • kahl*	orange
portakal suyu *pohr • tah • kahl soo • yoo*	orange juice
rakı *rah • kih*	spirit made from distilled grapes and aniseed, similar to French pastis or Lebanese arak
reçel *reh • chehl*	jam
ringa balığı *reen • gah bah • lih • ih*	herring [whitebait]
safran *sahf • rahn*	saffron
sahanda *sah • hahn • dah*	fried
salep *sah • lehp*	hot herbal drink
sarı şalgam *sah • rih shahl • gahm*	rutabaga [swede]

armısak *hr • mih • sahk*	garlic
bze çorbası *hb • zeh chohr • bah • sih*	vegetable soup
ek şarap *hk shah • rahp*	dry
ğır eti *h • ihr eh • tee*	beef
ğır filetosu *h • ihr fee • leh • toh • soo*	sirloin
da *h • dah*	soda
ğan *h • ahn*	onion
ğan çorbası *h • ahn chohr • bah • sih*	onion soup
sis *h • sees*	sausage
lün *u • lyun*	pheasant
t *ut*	milk
tlaç *ut • lahch*	rice pudding
tlü *ut • lyu*	with milk
tlü meyve suyu *ut • lyu may • veh soo • yoo*	milk shake
tsüz *ut • syuz*	black
lgam *ahl • gahm*	turnip
lgam suyu *ahl • gahm soo • yoo*	turnip juice

şarap listesini
shah • rahp lees • teh • see

şeftali
shehf • tah • lee

şeker
sheh • kehr

şekerli
sheh • kehr • lee

şıra
shih • rah

şiş köfte
sheesh kurf • teh

şişe
shee • sheh

tarama
tah • rah • mah

tatlı şarap
taht • lih shah • rahp

tavşan
tahv • shahn

tavuk
tah • vook

tavuk çorbası
tah • vook chohr • bah • sih

tavuk göğsü
tah • vook gur • hsyu

taze fasulye
tah • zeh fah • sool • yeh

taze soğan
tah • zeh soh • ahn

tereyağı
teh • reh • yah • ih

wine list	
peach	
sugar	
with sugar	
freshly pressed grape juice	
ground lamb croquettes on a skewer, grilled over charcoal	
bottle	
taramasalata, fish roe pâté	
sweet	
rabbit	
chicken	
chicken soup	
milk pudding with thin filaments of chicken breast	
green beans	
shallot [spring onion]	
butter	

on balığı _ohn_ bah • lih • _ih_	tuna
ulum peyniri oo • _loom_ pay • nee • _ree_	goat cheese
ürlü vur • _lyu_	cooked mixed vegetables and beans, served hot
skumru pilakisi os • _koom_ • roo pee • lah • kee • see	mackerel fried in olive oil, with potatoes, celery, carrots and garlic
züm u • _zyum_	grapes
ski ees • _kee_	whisky
otka oht • _kah_	vodka
apay tatlandırıcı ah • _pie_ taht • _lahn_ • dih • rih • jih	artificial sweetener
ğurtlu kebab oh • oort • _loo_ keh • _bahb_	kebab on toasted bread with pureed tomatoes and seasoned yogurt
murta oo • _moor_ • tah	egg

GOING OUT

GOING OUT 218
ROMANCE 222

GOING OUT

NEED TO KNOW

What is there to do in the evenings?	**Geceleri ne yapılır?** *geh • jeh • leh • <u>ree</u> neh yah • pih • lihr*
Do you have a program of events?	**Bir rehberiniz var mı?** *beer reh • beh • ree • <u>neez</u> vahr mih*
What's playing at the movies [cinema] tonight?	**Bu gece hangi filmler oynuyor?** *boo geh • <u>jeh</u> hahn • gee feelm • lehr oy • <u>noo</u> • yohr*
Where's…?	**Nerede…?** *neh • reh • deh…*
the downtown area	**kent merkezi** *<u>kehnt</u> mehr • keh • zee*
the bar	**bar** *bahr*
the dance club	**diskotek** *dees • koh • <u>tehk</u>*
Is there a cover charge?	**Giriş ücretli mi?** *gee • <u>reesh</u> yuj • reht • <u>lee</u> mee*

Culturally, Turkey has a lot to offer. There are numerous archeological sites spread throughout the country, which represent many different periods in history. The ruins at Efes (Ephesus), for example, are certainly worth a trip. Though the area was inhabited over 6000 years ago, during the Neolithic period, and traces have been excavated from various periods since then, the well-conserved ruins you can visit today are mainly from Roman times, that is, they are more than 2000 years old.

Moreover, there is no shortage of theaters, operas, concert halls and museums, particularly in the larger cities. And many cities in Turkey are host to excellent music, film and dance festivals throughout the year. Visit the local **Turizm Danışma Bürosu** (tourist information offices) to find out what's going on while you are in town.

ENTERTAINMENT

Can you recommend...?	**...önerebilir misiniz?** ... ur • neh • reh • bee • _leer_ mee • see • neez
a concert	**Konser** kohn • _sehr_
a movie	**Film** feelm
an opera	**Opera** oh • _peh_ • rah
a play	**Tiyatro oyunu** tee • _yaht_ • roh oh • _yoo_ • noo
When does it start/end?	**Ne zaman başlıyor/bitiyor?** _neh_ zah • _mahn_ bahsh • _lih_ • yohr/ bee • _tee_ • yohr

What's the dress code?	**Giyim tarzı ne?**
	gee • _yeem_ tahr • _zih_ neh
I like...	**...severim.**
	...seh • _veh_ • reem
classical music	**Klasik müzik**
	klah • _seek_ myu • _zeek_
folk music	**Halk müziği**
	hahlk myu • zee • _yee_
jazz	**Caz**
	jahz
pop music	**Pop**
	pohp
rap	**Rep**
	rehp

For Tickets, see page 45.

NIGHTLIFE

What is there to do in the evenings?	**Geceleri ne yapılır?**
	geh • jeh • leh • _ree neh yah_ • pih • lihr
Can you recommend...?	**...önerebilir misiniz?**
	...ur • neh • reh • bee • _leer_ mee • see • ne

a bar	**Bar**
	bahr
a casino	**Kumarhane**
	koo • mahr • hah • <u>neh</u>
a dance club	**Diskotek**
	<u>dees</u> • koh • tehk
a gay club	**Eşcinsel klübü**
	<u>ehsh</u> • jeen • sehl klyu • <u>byu</u>
a nightclub	**Gece klübü**
	geh • <u>jeh</u> klyu • <u>byu</u>
there live music?	**Orada canlı müzik var mı?**
	<u>oh</u> • rah • dah <u>jahn</u> • lih myu • <u>zeek</u> vahr mih
ow do I get there?	**Oraya nasıl gidebilirim?**
	<u>oh</u> • rah • yah <u>nah</u> • sihl
	gee • deh • bee • lee • reem
there a cover	**Masa ücreti var mı?**
ght?	*mah • <u>sah</u> yuj • reh • <u>tee</u> <u>vahr</u> mih*
et's go dancing.	**Hadi dans etmeye gidelim.**
	hah • <u>dee</u> dans eht • meh • yeh
	gee • deh • <u>leem</u>
this area safe at	**Bu bölge gece güvenli midir?**
ght?	*boo burl • geh geh • jeh gyu • vehn • lih*
	mih • deer

r The Dating Game, see page 222.

ROMANCE

NEED TO KNOW

Would you like to go out for a drink/meal?	**Dışarı çıkıp birşeyler içmek/yemek ister misiniz?** *dih • shah • rih chih • kihp beer shay • lehr eech • mehk/yeh • mehk ees • tehr mee • see • neez*
What are your plans for tonight/tomorrow?	**Bu gece/yarın için planınız ne?** *boo geh • jeh/yah • rinn ee • cheen plah • nih • nihz neh*
Can I have your number?	**Telefon numaranızı öğrenebilir miyim?** *teh • leh • fohn noo • mah • rah • nih • zih ur • reh • neh • bee • leer mee • yeem*
Can I join you?	**Size katılabilir miyim?** *see • zeh kah • tih • lah • bee • leer mee • yeem*
Let me buy you a drink.	**Size bir içki ısmarlayayım.** *see • zeh beer eech • kee ihs • mahr • lah • yah • yihm*
I like you.	**Sizden hoşlanıyorum.** *seez • dehn hohsh • lah • nih • yoh • room*
I love you.	**Sizi seviyorum.** *see • zee seh • vee • yoh • room*

THE DATING GAME

Would you like to…?	**…ister misiniz?** *…ees • tehr mee • see • neez*
go out for coffee	**Kahve içmeye gitmek** *kah • veh eech • meh • yeh geet • mehk*

go for a drink	**İçki içmeye gitmek**
	eech • kee eech • meh • yeh geet • mehk
go for a meal	**Yemeğe çıkmak**
	yeh • meh • yeh chihk • mahk
You're very attractive!	**Çok iyi görünüyorsunuz!**
	chohk ee • yee
	gur • ryu • nyu • yohr • soo • nooz
What are your plans for...?	**...için planınız ne?**
	...ee • cheen plah • nih • nihz neh
tonight	**Bu gece**
	boo geh • jeh
tomorrow	**Yarın**
	yah • rihn
this weekend	**Bu haftasonu**
	boo hahf • tah • soh • noo
Where would you like to go?	**Nereye gitmek istersiniz?**
	neh • reh • yeh geet • mehk
	ees • tehr • see • neez
I'd like to go to...	**...gitmek isterim.**
	...geet • mehk ees • teh • reem
Do you like...?	**...ister misiniz?**
	...ees • tehr mee • see • neez

Can I have your number/e-mail?	**Numaranızı/Posta adresinizi alabilir miyim?**
	noo • mah • rah • nih • zih/pohs • tah
	ahd • reh • see • nee • zee
	ah • lah • bee • leer mee • yeem
Are you on Facebook/ Twitter?	**Facebook/Twitter'da mısın?**
	Facebook/Twitter'dah
	mih • sihn
Can I join you?	**Size katılabilir miyim?**
	see • zeh kah • tih • lah • bee • leer
	mee • yeem
Shall we go somewhere quieter?	**Daha sakin bir yere gidelim mi?**
	dah • hah sah • keen
	beer yeh • reh gee • deh • leem mee

For Communications, see page 85.

ACCEPTING & REJECTING

Thank you. I'd love to.	**Teşekkür ederim. Sevinirim.**
	teh • shehk • kyur eh • deh • reem
	seh • vee • nee • reem
Where shall we meet?	**Nerede buluşalım?**
	neh • reh • deh boo • loo • shah • lihm
I'll meet you at the bar/ your hotel.	**Sizi barda/otelinizde bulurum.**
	see • zee bahr • dah/
	oh • teh • lee • neez • deh boo • loo • room
I'll come by at…	**…uğrarım.**
	…oo • rah • rihm
What's your address?	**Adresin nedir?**
	ahd • reh • seen neh • deer
Thank you, but I'm busy.	**Teşekkür ederim ama meşgulüm.**
	teh • shehk • kyur eh • deh • reem ah • ma
	mehsh • goo • lyum
I'm not interested.	**İlgilenmiyorum.**
	eel • gee • lehn • mee • yoh • room

Leave me alone!	**Beni yalnız bırakın lütfen!**
	beh • <u>nee</u> yahl • nihz bih • <u>rah</u> • kihn
	<u>lyut</u> • fehn
Stop bothering me!	**Canımı sıkmayı kesin!**
	jah • nih • <u>mih</u> sihk • mah • <u>yih</u> keh • seen

For Time, see page 23.

GETTING INTIMATE

Can I hug/kiss you?	**Sizi kucaklayabilir/öpebilir miyim?**
	see • <u>zee</u> koo • jahk • <u>lah</u> • yah • bee • <u>leer</u>/
	ur • peh • bee • <u>leer</u> mee • yeem
Yes.	**Evet.**
	<u>eh</u> • veht
No.	**Hayır.**
	<u>hah</u> • yihr
Stop!	**Dur!**
	door

SEXUAL PREFERENCES

Are you gay?	**Gey misiniz?**
	<u>gay</u> mee • see • neez
I'm heterosexual.	**Ben karşı cinse ilgi duyarım.**
	behn kahr • <u>shih</u> jeen • <u>seh</u> eel • <u>gee</u>
	doo • <u>yah</u> • rihm
I'm homosexual.	**Eşcinselim.**
	ehsh • jeen • <u>seh</u> • leem
I'm bisexual.	**Biseksüelim.**
	beeh • sehk • syu • <u>eh</u> • leem
Do you like men/	**Erkeklerden/Kadınlardan hoşlanır**
women?	**mısınız?**
	ehr • kehk • lehr • <u>dehn</u>/
	kah • dihn • lahr • <u>dahn hosh</u> • lah • <u>nihr</u>
	mih • sih • nihz

DICTIONARY

ENGLISH–TURKISH 228
TURKISH–ENGLISH 256

ENGLISH–TURKISH

A

abroad *adv* yurtdışı
accept *v* kabul etmek
accident kaza
accompany *v* eşlik etmek
acetaminophen
  parasetamol
acne sivilce
adapter adaptör
address adres
after sonra
air conditioner klima
air sickness bag sıhhi
  torba
airmail uçak ile
airport *n* havaalanı
aisle seat koridor kenarı
  koltuk
alarm clock çalar saat
all hepsi
allergy alerji
allow *v* izin vermek

allowance (customs)
  gümrüksüz geçebilecek
  miktar
almost neredeyse
alone yalnız
already zaten
also ayrıca
alter *v* değiştirmek
alternate route alternatif
  yol
aluminum foil
  alimünyum kağıtı
always her zaman
amazing hayret verici
ambassador elçi
ambulance ambülans
American *adj* Amerikan;
  n Amerikalı
amount (money) tutar
amusement park oyun
  parkı
animal hayvan

adj adjective	**BE** British English	**prep** preposition
adv adverb	**n** noun	**v** verb

another başka bir
antacid mide asidine
  karşı ilaç
antibiotics antibiyotik
antifreeze antifriz
antique (object) antika
antiseptic *adj* antiseptik
antiseptic cream
  antiseptik krem
anyone biri
apartment apartman
  dairesi
apologize *v* özür dilemek
appetite *n* iştah
appointment randevu
April Nisan
area code alan kodu
arcade oyun salonu
around (place) yakınları;
  (time) civarında
arrival (terminal) varış
arrive *v* varmak
art gallery sanat galerisi
arthritis *n* arterit
ask istemek
aspirin aspirin
assistance yardım
asthma astım

ATM paramatik
attack saldırı
attractive cazip
audio guide teybe
  alınmış rehber
August Ağustos
Australia Avustralya
authenticity hakikilik
automatic car otomatik
  araba
autumn [BE] sonbahar

B

baby bebek
baby bottle biberon
baby food bebek maması
baby wipes bebek
  mendili
babysitter çocuk bakıcısı
back (part of body) sırt
backpack sırt çanta
backache sırt ağrısı
bad kötü
bag çanta
baggage [BE] bavul
baggage cart alış veriş
  arabası
baggage check emanet

baggage claim bavul teslim bandi

baggage trolley [BE] alış veriş arabası

ball top

bandage bandaj

bank banka

bar bar

basket sepet

basketball basketbol

basketball game basketbol maçı

bathroom tuvalet

battery (vehicle) akü; (radio, watch) pil

battle site savaş meydanı

be v olmak

beach plaj

beautiful adj güzel

bed yatak

before önce

begin v başlamak

behind arkasında

belt kemer

bet n bahis

between (time) arasında

bicycle bisiklet

big büyük

bikini bikini

bill [BE] fatura; (receipt at restaurant) hesap

birthday doğum günü

bite (insect) sokmak

black adj siyah

blanket battaniye

blister su toplanması

blood pressure tansiyon

blouse bluz

blue mavi

boat trip tekne gezisi

book n kitap

book store kitapçı

boots bot; (sport) çizme

boring adj sıkıcı

botanical garden botanik bahçesi

bottle şişe

bottle opener şişe açacağı

box kutu

boxing match boks maç

boy erkek çocuk

boyfriend erkek arkadaş

bra sütyen
break v kırmak
breast meme
breathe v nefes almak
bridge köprü
briefs külot
bring v getirmek
Britain Britanya
British Britanyalı
brooch broş
broom süpürge
bus otobüs
bus station otobüs garajı
bus stop otobüs durağı
business iş
business center iş
merkezi
busy kalabalık
but ama
buy v satın almak

able car teleferik
afe kafe
alendar takvim
all v çağırmak;
(telephone) aramak

call collect karşı tarafa
ödetmek
camera fotoğraf makinesi
camp v kamp yapmak
campsite n kamp alanı
can opener konserve
açacağı
Canada Kanada
cancel v iptal etmek
car araba; **(train
compartment)** vagon
car park [BE] otopark
car rental araba kiralama
car seat araba koltuğu
carafe n sürahi
carpet (rug) halı
carry-on el çantası
carton kutu
cash para; nakit
cash desk [BE] kasa
cashier kasa
casino kumarhane
castle kale
cat kedi
catch v **(bus)** yetişmek
cathedral katedral
cave mağara

cell phone cep telefonu
certificate belge
change n **(coins)**
  bozuk para; v **(alter)**
  değiştirmek; **(bus,**
  train) aktarma yapmak;
  (money) bozdurmak
changing facilities
  bebeğin altını
  değiştirecek yer
charcoal odun kömürü
charge ücret
cheap ucuz
check fatura; **(receipt at**
  restaurant) hesap
check in v check-in
  yaptırmak
check-in desk uçuş kaydi
  masasi
check out (hotel) otelden
  ayrılmak
checking account cari
  hesap
chemist [BE] eczane
chest pain göğüs ağrısı
child çocuk

child seat çocuk
  sandalyesi
child's cot [BE] çocuk
  yatağı
church kilise
cigar puro
cigarette sigara
cinema [BE] sinema
classical music klasik
  müzik
clean adj temiz; v
  temizlemek
cleaning supplies
  temizlik maddeleri
clear silmek
cliff uçurum
cling film [BE] plastik
  ambalaj kağıdı
clock saat
close (near) yakın; v
  kapanmak
clothing store elbise
  mağazası
club (golf) sopa
coach (long-distance
  bus) şehirlerarası
  otobüs

coat palto

code (area) kod

coin madeni para

cold *n* (flu) soğuk algınlığı; *adj* (temperature) soğuk

colleague meslektaş

collect *v* almak

color renk

comb tarak

come *v* gelmek

commission komisyon

company (business) şirket; (companionship) arkadaşlık

computer bilgisayar

concert konser

concert hall konser salonu

conditioner saç kremi

condom prezervatif

conference konferans

confirm *v* teyit etmek

consulate konsolosluk

contact *v* bağlantı kurmak

contact lens kontak lens

contain *v* içermek

convention hall kongre salonu

cook ahçı

cooking facility pişirme olanağı; mutfak

copper bakır

corkscrew şarap açacağı

cost *v* tutmak

cot bebek yatağı

cotton (fabric) pamuklu; (cotton wool) pamuk

cough öksürük

country ülke

country code ülke kodu

courier (guide) rehber

cover charge masa ücreti

cramps kramp

credit card kredi kartı

crib çocuk yatağı

cruise *n* deniz yolculuğu

crystal (quartz) kuartz

cup fincan

currency para birimi

currency exchange office döviz bürosu

current account [BE] cari hesap
curtain perde
customs gümrük
cut kesik
cycling race bisiklet yarışı

D

damage n hasar
dance n dans; v dans etmek
dance club diskotek
dangerous curve tehlikeli kavşak
day gün
deaf sağır
December Aralık
deck chair katlanabilir koltuk
declare v beyan etmek
deep derin
delay gecikme
denim kot kumaşı
dentist diş doktoru
denture protez
deodorant deodoran

depart v (train, bus) kalkmak
department store mağaza
departure gate çıkış kapisi
deposit ön ödeme
desert çöl
detergent deterjan
diabetic (person) şeker hastası
diamond elmas
diaper bebek bezi
diarrhea ishal
dictionary sözlük
die ölmek
diesel dizel
difficult zor
directory (telephone) rehber
dirty kirli
disabled [BE] özürlü
discount indirim
dish (utensil) tabak çanak
dishwasher bulaşık makinesi

dishwashing liquid
bulaşık deterjanı
disposable razor tek
kullanımlık jilet
dive *v* dalmak
diving equipment dalış
donanımı
divorced boşanmış
do *v* yapmak
doctor doktor
doll bebek
dollar (U.S.) dolar
domestic flight iç hat
uçuşu
door kapı
double room çift kişilik
oda
downtown area kent
merkezi
dress elbise
dress code giyim tarzı
drive *v* seyretmek
driver sürücü
driver's license ehliyet
dry cleaner kuru
temizleyici
duty gümrük vergisi

duty-free goods vergisiz
eşyalar

E

earache kulak ağrısı
earrings küpe
east doğu
easy *adj* kolay
eat *v* yemek
economy class ekonomi
sınıfı
eight sekiz
eighteen on sekiz
eighty seksen
electrical outlet elektrik
prizi
electronic elektronik
elevator asansör
eleven on bir
e-mail *n* e-posta; *v*
yazmak
e-mail address e-posta
adresi
embassy elçilik
emergency acil durum
emergency exit acil çıkış

empty *adj* boş; *v*
  boşaltmak
end *v* bitmek
England İngiltere
English İngilizce
English-speaking
  İngilizce konuşan
enjoy *v* beğenmek
enter *v* girmek
equipment (sports)
  donanım
escalator yürüyen
  merdiven
e-ticket e-bilet
e-ticket check-in e-bilet
  kaydı
European Union AB
evening gece
excess luggage fazla
  bavul ağırlığı
exchange *v* değiştirmek
exchange rate döviz kuru
excursion gezinti
exit *n* çıkış; *v* çıkmak
expensive pahalı
expert uzman
express ekspres

extension dahili hat
extra (additional) daha
extra bed ek yatak
eye göz

F

fabric kumaş
facial yüz bakımı
fall sonbahar
family aile
fan (ventilator) vantilatör
far uzak
farm çiftlik
far-sighted yakını görme
  bozukluğu
fast (ahead) *adv* ileri;
  (speed) hızlı
fast-food restaurant
  hazır yemek lokantası
fax faks
February Şubat
fee komisyon
feed *v* yemek vermek
female kadın
ferry vapur
fever ateş
few birkaç tane

field tarla
fifteen on beş
fifty elli
fill *v* hazırlamak
fill up (car) doldurmak
filling (dental) dolgu
film film
find *v* bulmak
fine *adj* iyi
fire yangın
fire door yangin kapisi
fire extinguisher yangın söndürme aleti
first class birinci sınıf
fit *v* **(clothes)** olmak
fitting room soyunma odası
five beş
fix *v* onarmak
flat *adj* **(shoe)** patlak
flight uçuş
flight number uçuş numarası
floor (level) kat
fly *v* uçmak
folk music halk müziği
food yiyecek

football [BE] futbol
football game [BE] futbol maçı
foreign currency döviz
forest orman
fork çatal
form form
forty kırk
four dört
fourteen on dört
frame (glasses) çerçeve
free (available) boş; **(without charge)** ücretsiz
freezer dondurucu
fresh taze
Friday Cuma
friend arkadaş
full dolu

G

game (match) maç; **(toy)** oyun
garage (parking) garaj; **(repair)** araba tamirhanesi
garbage bag çöp torbası

garden bahçe
gas benzin
gas station benzin
   istasyonu
gate (airport) biniş kapısı
get v (find) bulmak
get a refund v para geri
   almak
get off v (bus, etc.)
   inmek
get to v gitmek
gift shop hediyelik eşya
   dükkanı
girl kız çocuk
girlfriend kız arkadaş
give v vermek
glass bardak
glasses (optical) gözlük
go v gitmek
gold altın
golf golf
golf club golf sopası
golf course golf sahası
golf tournament golf
   turnuvası
good adj iyi
green yeşil

grocery store bakkal
ground (earth) zemin
ground-floor room
   zemin-kat odası
guide (telephone) [BE]
   rehber; (tour) gezi
   rehberi
guide dog rehber köpeği
guide book rehber kitabı
gym jimnastik
gynecologist kadın
   hastalıkları uzmanı

H

hair saç
hairbrush saç fırçası
haircut saç tıraşı
hairdresser kuaför
hairspray saç spreyi
half adj yarım
hand el
handbag [BE] cüzdan
handicapped özürlü
happen v olmak
harbor liman
hard (difficult) zorlu;
   (solid) sert

hat şapka
have v sahip olmak
hear v duymak
heart kalp
heat n ısıtıcı
heater ısıtıcı
heating [BE] n ısıtıcı
heavy ağır
helmet kask
help yardım
here burada
high yüksek
highchair yüksek
  sandalye
highway otoyol
hill tepe
hire [BE] v kiralamak
hold on v (wait)
  beklemek
holiday [BE] tatil
home ev
horsetrack at yarışı
hospital hastane
hot sıcak
hotel otel
hour saat
house ev

how nasıl
hundred yüz
hungry aç
hurt v acımak
husband koca

I

ibuprofen ibuprofen
ice buz
identification kimlik
  belgesi
ill [BE] hasta
included dahil
incredible inanılmaz
indoor pool kapalı havuz
inexpensive ucuz
infection bulaşma
information bilgi
information desk
  danışma
  masası
information office
  danışma bürosu
innocent masum
insect böcek
insect bite böcek
  sokması

insect repellent böcek
  kovucu
inside içerde
instant messenger
  anında muhabbet
instruction kullanım
  talimatı
insurance sigorta
interest (hobby) ilgi alanı
interesting ilginç
intermediate orta
  seviyede
international flight diş
  hat uçuşu
internet internet
internet cafe internet
  kafe
internet service internet
  hizmeti
interpret tercüme etmek
interpreter tercüman
intersection kavşak
Ireland İrlanda
iron ütü
item eşya
itemized bill dökümlü
  hesap

J

jacket monta
January Ocak
jazz caz
jeans kot pantalon
jet-ski jet ski
jeweler kuyumcu
jewelry mücevherat
job iş
join v **(accompany)**
  katılmak; **(to get
  involved)** girmek
July Temmuz
June Haziran

K

key anahtar
key ring anahtarlık
kiddie pool çocuk havuzu
kilometer kilometre
kiss v öpmek
kitchen mutfak
kitchen foil [BE]
  alimünyum
  kağıtı
know v bilmek

L

lace dantel
lake göl
land v (airplane) inmek
large büyük
last adj son; sonuncu; v
devam etmek
late geç
aunderette [BE]
çamaşırhane
aundromat çamaşırhane
aundry facility
çamaşırhane
awyer avukat
eather deri
eave v (depart) kalkmak;
(deposit) bırakmak; (go)
gitmek
eft (side) sol
eg bacak
ens (camera) objektif;
(glasses) cam
etter mektup
brary kitaplık
fe boat cankurtaran
sandalı
fe jacket can yeleği

lifeguard cankurtaran
lift [BE] asansör
lift pass teleferik pasosu
light n (electric) ışık;
adj (not dark) aydınlık;
(not heavy) hafif; (color)
açık; (on vehicle) far
light bulb ampul
lighter (cigarette)
çakmak
like v beğenmek
line (subway) hat
linen keten
liquor store tekel bayii
lira (Turkish currency,
YTL) lira
liter litre
little (small) küçük
live v yaşamak
live music canlı müzik
local yerel
lock kilit
log on v girmek
login giriş
logout n çıkış; v çıkmak
long uzun
look like v benzemek

lose v kaybetmek
love v **(like)** beğenmek;
  (somebody) sevmek
low düşük
low bridge alçak köprü
luggage bavul
luggage cart el arabası
luggage locker bagaj
  dolapı

M

machine washable
  makinede yıkanabilir
magazine dergi
magnificent muhteşem
mail mektup
mailbox posta kutusu
main ana; başlıca
make-up n makyaj; v
  (a prescription) [BE]
  hazırlamak
male (man) erkek
mall alış veriş merkezi
manager müdür
manicure manikür
manual (car) el kitabı
map harita

March Mart
market pazar
mascara rimel
massage masaj
May Mayıs
match (smoking) kibrit;
  (sports) maç
measurement ölçü
medicine (medication)
  ilaç
medium (size) orta
meet v buluşmak
meeting toplantı
meeting room toplantı
  odası
message mesaj
microwave mikrodalga
midnight gece yarısı
mistake yanlışlık
mobile phone [BE] cep
  telefonu
moisturizer (cream)
  nemlendirici
moment an
Monday Pazartesi
money para
month ay

mop yer bezi
moped mopet
mosque cami
motion sickness yol tutması
motorboat motorlu tekne
motorcycle motorsiklet
motorway [BE] otoyol
mountain dağ
mouth ağız
move v taşınmak
movie film
movie theater sinema
movies theater sinema
mugging hırsızlık
museum müze
music müzik

nail file tırnak törpüsü
name isim
napkin peçete
nappy [BE] bebek bezi
national ulusal
near yakın
necklace kolye
new yeni

New Zealand Yeni Zelanda
newspaper gazete
newsstand gazete bayii
next (following) bir sonraki
next to yanında
nice iyi
nightclub gece klübü
nine dokuz
nineteen on dokuz
ninety doksan
non-smoking sigara içilmeyen
north kuzey
nose burun
nothing hiçbir şey
notify v bildirmek
November Kasım
novice acemi
number numara
nurse hemşire

O

October Ekim
office ofis

office hours çalışma
   saatleri
off-licence [BE] tekel
   bayii
off-peak kalabalık saatler
   dışında
often sık sık
old (senior) yaşlı; **(thing)**
   eski
one bir
one way tek yön
one-way ticket sırf gidiş
open adj açık; v **(store)**
   açılmak; v **(a window)**
   açmak
opening hours açılış
   saatleri
opera opera
opposite karşıda;
   karşısında
optician göz doktoru
orange (color) portakal
   rengi
order v sipariş vermek
outdoor açık havada
outdoor pool açık havuz
outside dışında; dışarda

overlook hakim tepe

P

pacifier emzik
pack v hazırlamak
package paket
paddling pool [BE] çocuk
   havuzu
pain acı
palace saray
pants pantalon
pantyhose tayt
paper towels kağıt
   havlusu
paracetamol [BE]
   parasetamol
park park
parking park yeri
parking lot otopark
party (social) parti
pass v **(a place)** geçmek
pass through geçmek
passport pasaport
passport control
   pasaport kontrolu
pastry store pastane
path patika

pay v ödemek
payment ödeme
peak tepe
pedestrian crossing
  yaya geçidi
pediatrician çocuk
  doktoru
people insanlar
period (menstrual)
  aybaşı
person kişi
petrol [BE] benzin
petrol station [BE]
  benzin istasyonu
pewter kurşun-kalay
  alaşımı
pharmacy eczane
phone n telefon; v telefon
  etmek
phone call telefon
  görüşmesi
phone card telefon kartı
photocopy fotokopi
photograph fotoğraf
phrase book konuşma
  kılavuzu
pick up v almak

picnic area piknik alanı
piece (item) parça
pill hap; (contraceptive)
  doğum kontrol hapı
pillow yastık
pillow case yastık kılıfı
PIN pin numarası
piste [BE] pist
place yer
plane uçak
plaster [BE] bandaj
plastic wrap plastik
  ambalaj kağıdı
plate tabak
platform [BE] peron
platinum platin
play n (theater) tiyatro
  oyunu; v (game)
  oynamak; (music)
  çalmak
playground çocuk parkı
plunger plançer
pocket cep
pole kayak sopası
point v (to something)
  göstermek
police polis

police report polis raporu
police station polis karakolu
pond gölcük
pop music pop
port (harbor) liman
post [BE] *n* posta; *v* postaya vermek
postbox [BE] posta kutusu
post office [BE] postane
postcard kartpostal
pottery çanak çömlek
pound (sterling) İngiliz sterlini
pregnant hamile
prescription reçete
press *v* ütülemek
price fiyat
problem soru
program program
purple mor
purpose sebeb
purse cüzdan
push chair [BE] puşet
put *v* koymak

Q
quarter çeyrek
quiet sessiz

R
racetrack hipodrom
racket (tennis, squash) raket
railway station [BE] tren garı
raincoat yağmurluk
rainy yağmurlu
rap rep
rape tecavüz
rash kaşıntı
razor jilet
razor blades jilet
ready hazır
real (genuine) gerçek; hakiki
receipt fatura; fiş
recommend *v* önermek
refrigerator buzdolabı
region bölge
regular (gas) normal; **(size)** orta boy
religion din

rent v kiralamak

epair v onarmak

epeat v tekrarlamak; tekrar etmek

eport v (crime) haber vermek

eservation yer ayırtmak

eserve (a table) v ayırtmak

estaurant lokanta

estroom tuvalet

eturn (ticket) [BE] gidiş dönüş; v (come back) dönmek; (surrender) bırakmak

ght (correct) doğru

ng yüzük

ver ırmak

ad yol

ad map yol haritası

bbery soygun

mantic romantik

om oda

om service oda servisi

und (of game) tur

und-trip gidiş dönüş

ute yol

rubbish [BE] çöp

rubbish bag [BE] çöp torbası

S

safe n kasa; adj (not dangerous) güvenli

sales tax KDV

sandals sandalet

sanitary napkin kadın bağı

sanitary pad [BE] kadın bağı

Saturday Cumartesi

sauna sauna

saving (account) tasarruf hesap

scarf eşarp

schedule tarife

scissors makas

Scotland İskoçya

sea deniz

seat (theater, movies) yer; (train) koltuk

see v görmek; (witness) tanık olmak

sell v satmak

seminar seminer
send göndermek
senior citizen yaşlı
separately ayrı ayrı
September Eylül
service (church) ayin; **(to a customer)** servis
seven yedi
seventeen on yedi
seventy yetmiş
shampoo şampuan
sheet (bed) çarşaf
ship gemi
shirt (men's) gömlek
shoe ayakkabı
shoe store ayakkabı dükkânı
shopping area alış veriş merkezi
shopping centre [BE] alış veriş merkezi
short kısa
shorts şort
show v göstermek
shower duş
side effect yan etkisi
sick hasta

sightseeing tour tur
silk ipek
silver gümüş
single (ticket) [BE] sırf gidiş
single room tek kişilik oda
sit v oturmak
six altı
sixteen on altı
sixty altmış
size beden
skirt etek
skis kayak
slippers terlik
slow (behind) geri; **(speed)** yavaş
small küçük
smoking sigara içilen
smoking area sigara içilen yer
sneakers lastik ayakkabı
snorkel şnorkel
snorkeling equipment şnorkel takımı
snow n kar; v kar yağmak
snowboard kar kayağı

snowshoe kar ayakkabısı
snowy karlı
soap sabun
soccer futbol
soccer game futbol maçı
sock çorap
socket priz
some bazı
something bir şey
soon yakında
soother [BE] emzik
sore throat boğaz ağrısı
south güney
souvenir hediyelik eşya
souvenir guide hediyelik
  eşya rehberi
souvenir store hediyelik
  eşya dükkanı
speak v konuşmak;
  (language) bilmek
special özel
sport spor
sports massage spor
  masajı
sprain burkulma
spring ilkbahar
square (town) meydan

stadium stadyum
stairs merdivenler
stamp n **(postage)** pul; v
  mühürletmek
start v **(car)** çalıştırmak;
  (commence) başlamak
stay v kalmak
steep dik
stomach mide
stomachache mide ağrısı
stop n **(bus)** durak;
  (subway) metro
  istasyonu; v durmak
store mağaza
store directory mağaza
  rehberi
store guide [BE] mağaza
  rehberi
stove fırın
straight ahead doğru
  ilerde
strange şaşırtıcı
stream dere
strike v **(hit)** vurmak
stroller puşet
student öğrenci
study v okumak

summer yaz
Sunday Pazar
suppose sanmak
style üslup
subway metro
subway map metro planı
subway station metro
  istasyonu
suggest v önermek
suit takım elbise
suitable uygun
sun güneş
sunburn güneş yanığı
sunglasses güneş
  gözlüğü
sunny güneşli
sunscreen güneş
  geçirmez krem
sunstroke güneş
  çarpması
super (petrol) [BE] süper
superb mükemmel
supermarket
  süpermarket
suppository fitil
surfboard surf tahtası
sweater süveter

sweatshirt sweatshirt
swelling şişlik
swim v yüzmek
swimming pool yüzme
  havuzu
swimming trunks mayo
swimsuit mayo
synagogue havra

T

table masa
tablet tablet
take v (carry) götürmek;
  (medicine) almak;
  (room) tutmak; (time)
  binmek
take off çıkartmak
talk v konuşmak
tampon tampon
taxi taksi
taxi stand taksi durağı
team takım
tell v söylemek
ten on
tennis court tenis kortu
tennis match tenis maçı
tent çadır

terminal terminal
terrible berbat; kötü
that o
theft hırsızlık
thermal spring termal
  kaynağı
thick kalın
thief hırsız
thin ince
thirteen on üç
thirty otuz
this bu
three üç
throat boğaz
Thursday Perşembe
ticket bilet
ticket office bilet gişesi
tie kravat
tights [BE] tayt
time saat
timetable [BE] tarife
tissue kağıt mendil
tobacconist tütüncü
today bugün
toilet [BE] tuvalet
toilet paper tuvalet
  kağıdı

tomorrow *adv* yarın
too (extreme) çok
too much çok fazla
tooth diş
toothache diş ağrısı
toothbrush diş fırçası
toothpaste diş macunu
tour (sightseeing) tur
tourist turist
tourist office turist
  danışma bürosu
towel havlu
town şehir; kent
town map kent haritası
town square kasaba
  meydanı
toy store oyuncakçı
track peron
traditional geleneksel
traffic light trafik ışığı
trail pist
trail map pist haritası
train tren
train station tren garı
trash çöp
travel agency seyahat
  acentası

travel sickness [BE] yol tutması
traveler's check seyahat çeki
traveller's cheque [BE] seyahat çeki
trim uçlarından alma
trip yolculuk; gezi
trousers [BE] pantalon
try on v (clothes) denemek
T-shirt tişört
Tuesday Salı
tunnel tünel
Turkey Türkiye
Turkish (language) Türkçe; **(nationality)** Türk
turn off v kapatmak
turn on v açmak
TV televizyon
twelve on iki
twenty yirmi
two iki
typical tipik

U

ugly çirkin
umbrella şemsiye
under altında
underground [BE] metro
underground map [BE] metro planı
underground station [BE] metro istasyonu
underpants [BE] külot
understand v anlamak
United Kingdom Birleşik Krallık
United States of America Amerika Birleşik Devletleri
unlimited mileage sınırsız yakıt kullanımı
until kadar
upset stomach mide bozukluğu
urgent acil
use v kullanmak

V

vacation tatil
vacation resort tatil yeri

cuum cleaner elektrikli
süpürge

ginal infection vajina
tihabı

lley vadi

lue değer

T [BE] KDV

getarian (meal) etsiz;
person) vejetaryen

ry çok

lage köy

heyard bağ

sa vize

sit n ziyaret; v ziyaret
tmek

siting hours ziyaret
aatleri

lleyball voleybol

lleyball game voleybol
naçı

mit v kusmak

it v beklemek

iter garson

itress garson

wake (someone)
uyandırmak

wake-up call arama
uyandirma

walking route yürüyüş
yolu

wallet cüzdan

warm ılık

washing machine
çamaşır makinesi

watch (wrist) kol saati

water su

water skis su kayağı

waterfall şelale

way yol

weather hava

weather forecast hava
tahmini

Wednesday Çarşamba

weekend rate hafta sonu
fiyatı

west batı

what ne

wheelchair tekerlekli
sandalye

wheelchair ramp
tekerlekli sandalye
rampası
when ne zaman
where nerede
who kim
why niçin
wife karı
**window (office,
apartment)** pencere
window case vitrin
window seat pencere
kenarı koltuk
windsurfer rüzgar
sörfçüsü
winery şaraphane
wireless internet
kablosuz internet
winter kış
withdraw funds çekilen
paralar
within (time) içinde
wool yün
work v **(function)**
çalışmak
wrong yanlış

Y
yield yol vermek
youth hostel gençlik
yurdu

Z
zero sıfır
zoo hayvanat bahçesi

TURKISH–ENGLISH

A

AB European Union
acemi novice
acı pain
acımak hurt *v*
acil urgent
acil çıkış emergency exit
acil durum emergency
aç hungry
açık open *adj*; light *adj* (color)
açık havada outdoor
açık havuz outdoor pool
açılış saatleri opening hours
açılmak open *v* (store)
açmak open *v* (a window); turn on
adaptör adapter
adres address
ağır heavy
ağız mouth
Ağustos August
ahçı cook
aile family

aktarma yapmak change *v* (bus, train)
akü battery (vehicle)
alan kodu area code
alçak köprü low bridge
alış veriş arabası baggage cart [trolley BE]
alerji allergy
alış veriş merkezi mall [shopping centre BE]; shopping area
alimünyum kağıtı aluminum [kitchen BE] foil
almak collect *v*; pick up; take (medicine)
altı six
altın gold
altında under
alternatif yol alternate route
altmış sixty
ama but
ambülans ambulance

Amerika Birleşik Devletleri United States of America
Amerikalı American n
Amerikan American adj
ampul light bulb
an moment
ana main
anahtar key
anahtarlık key ring
anında muhabbet instant messenger
anlamak understand v
antibiyotik antibiotics
antifriz antifreeze
antika antique (object)
antiseptik antiseptic
antiseptik krem antiseptic cream
apartman dairesi apartment
araba car
araba kiralama car rental
araba koltuğu car seat
araba tamirhanesi garage (repair)

Aralık December
aramak call v (telephone)
arama-uyandirma wake-up call
arasında between (time)
arkadaş friend
arkadaşlık company (companionship)
arkasında behind
arterit arthritis
asansör elevator [lift BE]
aspirin aspirin
astım asthma
at yarışı horsetrack
ateş fever
avukat lawyer
Avustralya Australia
ay month
ayakkabı shoe
ayakkabı dükkânı shoe store
aybaşı period (menstrual)
aydınlık bright adj (not dark)
ayırtmak reserve v (a table)
ayrı ayrı separately

ayrıca also
ayin service (church)

B

bacak leg
bagaj dolapı luggage
  locker
bağ vineyard
bağlantı kurmak
  contact v
bahçe garden
bahis bet n
bakır copper
bakkal grocery store
bandaj bandage [plaster
  BE]
banka bank
bar bar
bardak glass
basketbol basketball
basketbol maçı
  basketball game
başka bir another
başlamak begin v; start
  (commence)
başlıca main
batı west
battaniye blanket

bavul luggage [baggage
  BE]
bavul teslim bandi
  baggage claim
bazı some
bebeğin altını
  değiştirecek yer
  changing facilities
bebek baby; doll
bebek bezi diaper [nappy
  BE]
bebek maması baby food
bebek mendili baby
  wipes
bebek yatağı cot
beden size
beğenmek enjoy v; like
  v; love
beklemek hold on v; wait
belge certificate
benzemek look like v
benzin gas [petrol BE]
benzin istasyonu gas
  [petrol BE] station
berbat terrible
beş five
beyan etmek declare v

rakmak return v
surrender); leave
deposit)
beron baby bottle
kini bikini
ldirmek notify v
let ticket
let gişesi ticket office
lgi information
lgisayar computer
lmek know v; speak
language)
niş kapısı gate (airport)
nmek take v (time)
r one
r şey something
r sonraki next
following)
ri anyone
rinci sınıf first class
rkaç tane few
rleşik Krallık United
Kingdom
siklet bicycle
siklet yarışı cycling
ace
tmek end v
uz blouse

boğaz throat
boğaz ağrısı sore throat
boks maçı boxing match
boş free (available);
empty
boşaltmak empty v
boşanmış divorced
bot boots
botanik bahçesi
botanical garden
bozdurmak change v
(money)
bozuk para change n
(coins)
böcek insect
böcek kovucu insect
repellent
böcek sokması insect
bite
bölge region
Britanya Britain
Britanyalı British
broş brooch
bu this
bugün today
bulaşık deterjanı
dishwashing liquid

bulaşık makinesi dishwasher
bulaşma infection
bulmak find v; get
buluşmak meet v
burada here
burkulma sprain
burun nose
buz ice
buzdolabı refrigerator
büyük big; large

C

cam glasses
cami mosque
can yeleği life jacket
cankurtaran lifeguard
cankurtaran sandalı life boat
canlı müzik live music
cari hesap checking [current BE] account
caz jazz
cazip attractive
cep pocket
cep telefonu cell [mobile BE] phone

check-in yaptırmak check in v
civarında around (time)
Cuma Friday
Cumartesi Saturday
cüzdan purse [handbag BE]; wallet

Ç

çadır tent
çağırmak call v
çakmak lighter (cigarette)
çalar saat alarm clock
çalışma saatleri office hours
çalışmak work v (function)
çalıştırmak start v (car)
çalmak play v (music)
çamaşır makinesi washing machine
çamaşırhane laundromat [launderette BE]; laundry facility
çanak çömlek pottery
çanta bag
çarşaf sheet (bed)
Çarşamba Wednesday

çatal fork

çekilen paralar withdraw funds

çerçeve frame (glasses)

çeyrek quarter

çıkartmak take off

çıkış exit *n*; logout

çıkış kapisi departure gate

çıkmak exit *v*; logout

çift kişilik oda double room

çiftlik farm

çirkin ugly

çizme boots (sport)

çocuk child

çocuk bakıcısı babysitter

çocuk doktoru pediatrician

çocuk havuzu kiddie [paddling BE] pool

çocuk parkı playground

çocuk sandalyesi child seat

çocuk yatağı crib [child's cot BE]

çok too (extreme); very

çok fazla too much

çorap sock

çöl desert

çöp trash [rubbish BE]

çöp torbası garbage [rubbish BE] bag

D

dağ mountain

daha extra (additional)

dahil included

dahili hat extension

dalış donanımı diving equipment

dalmak dive *v*

danışma bürosu information office

danışma masası information desk

dans dance *n*

dans etmek dance *v*

dantel lace

değer value

değiştirmek change *v* (alter); alter; exchange

denemek try on *v* (clothes)

deniz sea

deniz yolculuğu cruise *n*

deodoran deodorant

dere stream

dergi magazine

deri leather

derin deep

deterjan detergent

devam etmek last *v*

dışarda outside

dışında outside

dik steep

din religion

diş tooth

diş ağrısı toothache

diş doktoru dentist

diş fırçası toothbrush

diş hat uçuşu international flight

diş macunu toothpaste

diskotek dance club

dizel diesel

doğru right (correct)

doğru ilerde straight ahead

doğu east

doğum günü birthday

doğum kontrol hapı pill (contraceptive)

doksan ninety

doktor doctor

dokuz nine

dolar dollar (U.S.)

doldurmak fill up (car)

dolgu filling (dental)

dolu full

donanım equipment (sports)

dondurucu freezer

dökümlü hesap itemized bill

dönmek return *v* (come back)

dört four

döviz foreign currency

döviz bürosu currency exchange office

döviz kuru exchange rate

durak stop *n* (bus)

durmak stop *v*

duş shower

duymak hear *v*

düşük low

E

e-bilet e-ticket

e-bilet kaydi e-ticket check-in

czane pharmacy
[chemist BE]
liyet driver's license
k yatak extra bed
kim October
konomi sınıfı economy
class
kspres express
hand
arabası luggage cart
trolley BE]
çantası carry-on
kitabı manual (car)
bise dress
bise mağazası clothing
store
çi ambassador
çilik embassy
ektrik prizi electrical
outlet
ektrikli süpürge
vacuum
cleaner
ektronik electronic
li fifty
mas diamond
nanet baggage check

emzik pacifier [soother
BE]
e-posta e-mail n
e-posta adresi e-mail
address
erkek male (man)
erkek arkadaş boyfriend
erkek çocuk boy
eski old (thing)
eşarp scarf
eşlik etmek accompany v
eşya item
etek skirt
etsiz vegetarian (meal)
ev home; house
Eylül September

F

faks fax
far light adj (on vehicle)
fatura receipt [bill BE]
fazla bavul ağırlığı
excess luggage
fırın stove
film film; movie
fincan cup
fiş receipt
fitil suppository

fiyat price
form form
fotoğraf photograph
fotoğraf makinesi camera
fotokopi photocopy
futbol soccer [football BE]
futbol maçı soccer [football BE] game

G

garaj garage (parking)
garson waiter; waitress
gazete newspaper
gazete bayii newsstand
gece evening
gece klübü nightclub
gece yarısı midnight
gecikme delay
geç late
geçmek pass v (a place); pass through
geleneksel traditional
gelmek come v
gemi ship
gençlik yurdu youth hostel
gerçek real (genuine)

geri slow (behind)
getirmek bring v
gezi trip
gezi rehberi guide (tour)
gezinti excursion
gidiş dönüş round-trip [return BE] (ticket)
giriş login
girmek enter v; log on; join (to get involved); get to; go; leave (go)
giyim tarzı dress code
golf golf
golf sahası golf course
golf sopası golf club
golf turnuvası golf tournament
göğüs ağrısı chest pain
göl lake
gölcük pond
gömlek shirt (men's)
göndermek send v
görmek see v
göstermek point v (to something); show
götürmek take v (carry)
göz eye
göz doktoru optician

zlük glasses (optical)
mrük customs
mrük vergisi duty
mrüksüz geçebilecek
ıiktar allowance
customs)
müş silver
n day
neş sun
neş çarpması
unstroke
neş geçirmez krem
unscreen
neş gözlüğü
unglasses
neş yanığı sunburn
néşli sunny
ney south
venli safe adj (not
angerous)
zel beautiful

ber vermek report v
rime)
fif light adj (not heavy)
fta sonu fiyatı
eekend rate

hakiki real (genuine)
hakikilik authenticity
hakim tepe overlook
halı carpet (rug)
halk müziği folk music
hamile pregnant
hap pill
harita map
hasar damage n
hasta sick [ill BE]
hastane hospital
hat line (subway)
hava weather
hava tahmini weather
  forecast
havaalanı airport
havlu towel
havra synagogue
hayret verici amazing
hayvan animal
hayvanat bahçesi zoo
hazır ready
hazır yemek lokantası
  fast-food restaurant
hazırlamak fill [make-up
  BE] (a prescription) v;
  pack
Haziran June

hediyelik eşya souvenir
hediyelik eşya dükkanı
  gift shop; souvenir store
hediyelik eşya rehberi
  souvenir guide
hemşire nurse
hepsi all
her zaman always
hesap check (receipt at
  restaurant, etc.)
hırsız thief
hırsızlık mugging; theft
hızlı fast (speed)
hiçbir şey nothing
hipodrom racetrack

I

ılık warm
ırmak river
ısıtıcı heat n; heater
  [heating BE]
ışık light n (electric)

i

ibuprofen ibuprofen
iç hat uçuşu domestic
  flight
içerde inside

içermek contain v
içinde within (time)
iki two
ilaç medicine
  (medication)
ileri fast (ahead)
ilgi alanı interest (hobby)
ilginç interesting
ilkbahar spring
inanılmaz incredible
ince thin
indirim discount
İngiliz sterlini pound
  (sterling)
İngilizce English
İngilizce konuşan
  English-speaking
İngiltere England
inmek get off v (bus);
  land (airplane)
insanlar people
internet internet
internet hizmeti internet
  service
internet kafe internet
  cafe
ipek silk
iptal etmek cancel v

İrlanda Ireland
ishal diarrhea
isim name
İskoçya Scotland
istemek ask
iş business; job
iş merkezi business
  center
ştah appetite
yi fine *adj*; good; nice
zin vermek allow

et ski jet-ski
ilet razor; razor blades
'mnastik gym

ablosuz internet
  wireless internet
abul etmek accept *v*
adar until
adın female
adın bağı sanitary
  napkin [pad BE]
adın hastalıkları
  uzmanı gynecologist
afe cafe

kağıt havlusu paper
  towels
kağıt mendil tissue
kalabalık busy
kalabalık saatler
  dışında off-peak
kale castle
kalın thick
kalkmak depart *v* (train,
  bus); leave (depart)
kalmak stay *v*
kalp heart
kamp alanı campsite
kamp yapmak camp *v*
Kanada Canada
kapalı havuz indoor pool
kapanmak close *v*; turn
  off
kapı door
kar snow *n*
kar ayakkabısı
  snowshoe
kar kayağı snowboard
kar yağmak snow *v*
karı wife
karlı snowy
karşı tarafa ödetmek
  call collect

karşıda opposite
karşısında opposite
kartpostal postcard
kasa cashier [cash desk BE]; safe
kasaba meydanı town square
Kasım November
kask helmet
kaşıntı rash
kat floor (level)
katedral cathedral
katılmak join v (accompany)
katlanabilir koltuk deck chair
kavşak intersection
kayak skis
kayak sopası pole
kaybetmek lose v
kaza accident
KDV sales tax [VAT BE]
kedi cat
kemer belt
kent town
kent haritası town map
kent merkezi downtown area

kesik cut
keten linen
kırk forty
kırmak break v
kısa short
kış winter
kız arkadaş girlfriend
kız çocuk girl
kibrit match (smoking)
kilise church
kilit lock
kilometre kilometer
kim who
kimlik belgesi identification
kiralamak rent [hire BE]
kirli dirty
kişi person
kitap book n
kitapçı bookstore
kitaplık library
klasik müzik classical music
klima air conditioner
koca husband
kod code (area)
kol saati watch (wrist)
kolay easy

koltuk seat (train)

kolye necklace

komisyon commission; fee

konferans conference

kongre salonu convention hall

konser concert

konser salonu concert hall

konserve açacağı can opener

konsolosluk consulate

kontak lens contact lens

konuşma kılavuzu phrase book

konuşmak talk v; speak

koridor kenarı koltuk aisle seat

kot kumaşı denim

kot pantalon jeans

koymak put v

köprü bridge

kötü terrible (weather); bad

köy village

kramp cramps

kravat tie

kredi kartı credit card

kuaför hairdresser

kuartz crystal (quartz)

kulak ağrısı earache

kullanım talimatı instruction

kullanmak use v

kumarhane casino

kumaş fabric

kurşun-kalay alaşımı pewter

kuru temizleyici dry cleaner

kusmak vomit v

kutu box; carton

kuyumcu jeweler

kuzey north

küçük little; small

külot briefs [underpants BE]

küpe earrings

L

lastik ayakkabı sneakers

liman harbor; port

lira (Turkish currency, YTL) lira

litre liter

lokanta restaurant

M

maç match (sports);
 game (match)
madeni para coin
mağara cave
mağaza store;
 department store
mağaza rehberi store
 directory [guide BE]
makas scissors
makinede yıkanabilir
 machine washable
makyaj make-up n
manikür manicure
Mart March
masa table
masa ücreti cover charge
masaj massage
masum innocent
mavi blue
Mayıs May
mayo swimming trunks;
 swimsuit
mektup letter; mail
meme breast
merdivenler stairs

mesaj message
meslektaş colleague
metro subway
 [underground
 BE]
metro istasyonu subway
 [underground] stop;
 subway [underground
 BE] station
metro planı subway
 [underground BE] map
meydan square (town)
mide stomach
mide ağrısı stomachache
mide asidine karşı ilaç
 antacid
mide bozukluğu upset
 stomach
mikrodalga microwave
monta jacket
mopet moped
mor purple
motorlu tekne motorboa
motorsiklet motorcycle
muhteşem magnificent
mutfak kitchen; cooking
 facility
mücevherat jewelry

müdür manager
mühürletmek stamp *v*
mükemmel superb
müze museum
müzik music

N

nakit cash *n*
nasıl how
ne what
ne zaman when
nefes almak breathe *v*
nemlendirici moisturizer (cream)
nerede where
neredeyse almost
niçin why
nisan April
normal regular (gas)
numara number

o that
objektif lens (camera)
ocak January
oda room
oda servisi room service
odun kömürü charcoal

ofis office
okumak study *v*
olmak be *v*; fit (clothes); happen
on ten
on altı sixteen
on beş fifteen
on bir eleven
on dokuz nineteen
on dört fourteen
on iki twelve
on sekiz eighteen
on üç thirteen
on yedi seventeen
onarmak fix *v*; repair
opera opera
orman forest
orta medium (size)
orta boy regular (size)
orta seviyede intermediate
otel hotel
otelden ayrılmak check out (hotel)
otobüs bus
otobüs durağı bus stop
otobüs garajı bus station

otomatik araba
automatic car
otopark parking lot [car park BE]
otoyol highway [motorway BE]
oturmak sit v
otuz thirty
oynamak play v (game)
oyun game (toy)
oyun parkı amusement park
oyun salonu arcade
oyuncakçı toy store

Ö

ödeme payment
ödemek pay v
öğrenci student
öksürük cough
ölçü measurement
ölmek die
ön ödeme deposit
önce before
önermek recommend v; suggest
öpmek kiss v
özel special

özür dilemek apologize v
özürlü handicapped [disabled BE]

P

pahalı expensive
paket package
palto coat
pamuk cotton (cotton wool)
pamuklu cotton (fabric)
pantalon pants [trousers BE]
para cash n; money
para birimi currency
para geri almak get a refund v
paramatik ATM
parasetamol acetaminophen [paracetamol BE]
parça piece (item)
park park
park yeri parking
parti party (social)
pasaport passport
pasaport kontrolu passport control

pastane pastry store
patika path
patlak *adj* flat (shoe)
pazar market
Pazar Sunday
Pazartesi Monday
peçete napkin
pencere window (office, apartment)
pencere kenarı koltuk window seat
perde curtain
peron track [platform BE]
Perşembe Thursday
piknik alanı picnic area
pil battery (radio, watch)
pin numarasi PIN
pişirme olanağı cooking facility
pist trail [piste BE]
pist haritası trail map
plaj beach
plançer plunger
plastik ambalaj kağıdı plastic wrap [cling film BE]
platin platinum
polis police

polis karakolu police station
polis raporu police report
pop pop music
portakal rengi orange (color)
posta mail *n* [post BE]
posta kutusu mailbox [postbox BE]
postane post office
postaya vermek mail *v* [post BE]
prezervatif condom
priz socket
program program
protez denture
pul stamp *n* (postage)
puro cigar
puşet stroller [push chair BE]

R

raket racket (tennis, squash)
randevu appointment
reçete prescription

rehber courier (guide); directory [guide BE] (telephone)

rehber kitabı guide book

rehber köpeği guide dog

renk color

rep rap

rimel mascara

romantik romantic

rüzgar sörfçüsü windsurfer

S

saat clock; hour; time

sabun soap

saç hair

saç fırçası hairbrush

saç kremi conditioner

saç spreyi hairspray

saç tıraşı haircut

sağır deaf

sahip olmak have v

saldırı attack

Salı Tuesday

sanat galerisi art gallery

sandalet sandals

sanmak suppose

saray palace

satın almak buy v

satmak sell v

sauna sauna

savaş meydanı battle site

sebeb purpose

sekiz eight

seksen eighty

seminer seminar

sepet basket

sert hard (solid)

servis service (to customer)

sessiz quiet

sevmek love v (somebody)

seyahat acentası travel agency

seyahat çeki traveler's check [cheque BE]

seyretmek drive v

sıcak hot

sıfır zero

sıhhi torba air sickness bag

sık sık often

sıkıcı boring

sınırsız yakıt kullanımı unlimited mileage

sırf gidiş one-way [single BE] ticket

sırt back (part of body)

sırt ağrısı backache

sırt çanta backpack

sigara cigarette

sigara içilen smoking

sigara içilen yer smoking area

sigara içilmeyen non-smoking

sigorta insurance

silmek clear

sinema movie theater [cinema BE]

sipariş vermek order v

sivilce acne

siyah black

soğuk cold adj (temperature)

soğuk algınlığı cold n (flu)

sokmak bite (insect)

sol left (side)

son last adj

sonbahar fall [autumn BE]

sonra after

sonuncu last adj

sopa club (golf)

soru problem

soygun robbery

soyunma odası fitting room

söylemek tell v

sözlük dictionary

spor sport

spor masajı sports massage

stadyum stadium

su water

su kayağı water skis

su toplanması blister

surf tahtası surfboard

süper super (gas [petrol BE])

süpermarket supermarket

süpürge broom

sürahi carafe

sürücü driver

sütyen bra

süveter sweater

sweatshirt sweatshirt

Ş

şampuan shampoo
şapka hat
şarap açacağı corkscrew
şaraphane winery
şaşırtıcı strange
şehir town
şehirlerarası otobüs
  coach (long-distance
  bus)
şeker hastası diabetic
  (person)
şelale waterfall
şemsiye umbrella
şirket company
  (business)
şişe bottle
şişe açacağı bottle
  opener
şişlik swelling
şnorkel snorkel
şnorkel takımı snorkeling
  equipment
şort shorts
Şubat February

T

tabak plate
tabak çanak dish
  (utensil)
tablet tablet
takım team
takım elbise suit
taksi taxi
taksi durağı taxi stand
takvim calendar
tampon tampon
tanık olmak see v
  (witness)
tansiyon blood pressure
tarak comb
tarife schedule
  [timetable BE]
tarla field
tasarruf hesap saving
  (account)
taşınmak move v
tatil vacation [holiday BE]
tatil yeri vacation resort
tayt pantyhose [tights BE]
taze fresh
tecavüz rape
tehlikeli kavşak
  dangerous curve

tek kişilik oda single room

tek kullanımlık jilet disposable razor

tek yön one way

tekel bayii liquor store [off-licence BE]

tekerlekli sandalye wheelchair

tekerlekli sandalye rampası wheelchair ramp

tekne gezisi boat trip

tekrar etmek repeat v

tekrarlamak repeat v

teleferik cable car

teleferik pasosu lift pass

telefon phone n

telefon etmek phone v

telefon görüşmesi phone call

telefon kartı phone card

televizyon TV

temiz clean

temizlemek clean v

temizlik maddeleri cleaning supplies

temmuz July

tenis kortu tennis court

tenis maçı tennis match

tepe hill; peak

tercüman interpreter

tercüme etmek interpret v

terlik slippers

termal kaynağı thermal spring

terminal terminal

teybe alınmış rehber audio guide

teyit etmek confirm v

tırnak törpüsü nail file

tipik typical

tişört T-shirt

tiyatro oyunu play n (theater)

top ball

toplantı meeting

toplantı odası meeting room

trafik ışığı traffic light

tren train

tren garı train [railway BE] station

tur round (of game); sightseeing tour

turist tourist
turist danışma bürosu tourist office
tutar amount (money)
tutmak take v (room); cost
tuvalet bathroom; restroom [toilet BE]
tuvalet kağıdı toilet paper
tünel tunnel
Türk Turkish (nationality)
Türkçe Turkish (language)
Türkiye Turkey
tütüncü tobacconist

U

ucuz cheap; inexpensive
uçak plane
uçak ile airmail
uçlarından alma trim
uçmak fly v
uçurum cliff
uçuş flight
uçuş kaydi masasi check-in desk
uçuş numarası flight number

ulusal national
uyandırmak wake (someone)
uygun suitable
uzak far
uzman expert
uzun long

Ü

ücret charge
ücretsiz free (without charge)
üç three
ülke country
ülke kodu country code
üslup style
ütü iron
ütülemek press v

V

vadi valley
vagon car (train compartment)
vajina iltihabı vaginal infection
vantilatör fan (ventilato
vapur ferry
variş arrival (terminal)

varmak arrive v

vejetaryen vegetarian
  (person)

vergisiz eşyalar duty-free
  goods

vermek give v

vitrin window (store);
  window case

vize visa

voleybol volleyball

voleybol maçı volleyball
  game

vurmak strike v (hit)

___

yağmurlu rainy

yağmurluk raincoat

yakın near; close (near)

yakında soon

yakını görme bozukluğu
  far-sighted

yakınları around (place)

yalnız alone

yan etkisi side effect

yangın fire

yangın kapisi fire door

yangın söndürme aleti
  fire extinguisher

yanında next to

yanlış wrong

yanlışlık mistake

yapmak do v

yardım help; assistance

yarım half adj

yarın tomorrow

yaşamak live v

yaşlı senior citizen; old
  adj (senior)

yastık pillow

yastık kılıfı pillow case

yatak bed

yavaş slow (speed)

yaya geçidi pedestrian
  crossing

yaz summer

yazmak e-mail v

yedi seven

yemek eat v

yemek vermek feed v

yeni new

Yeni Zelanda New
  Zealand

yer place; seat (theater,
  movies)

yer ayırtmak reservation

yer bezi mop

yerel local
yeşil green
yetişmek catch *v* (bus)
yetmiş seventy
yirmi twenty
yiyecek food
yol road; route; way
yol haritası road map
yol tutması motion [travel BE] sickness
yol vermek yield
yolculuk trip
yurtdışı abroad
yüksek high
yüksek sandalye highchair
yün wool
yürüyen merdiven escalator
yürüyüş yolu walking route
yüz hundred
yüz bakımı facial
yüzme havuzu swimming pool
yüzmek swim *v*
yüzük ring

Z

zaten already
zemin ground (earth)
zemin-kat odası ground-floor room
ziyaret visit *n*
ziyaret etmek visit *v*
ziyaret saatleri visiting hours
zor difficult
zorlu hard (difficult)